parents' lives, children's needs

working together for everyone's well-being

beth roy

PERSONHOOD PRESS

Parents' Lives, Children's Needs

PERSONHOOD PRESS

Published by
Personhood Press
P.O. Box 370
Fawnskin, CA 92333
800-429-1192
info@personhoodpress.com
www.personhoodpress.com

Library of Congress Control Number: 2007920746
ISBN 10: 1-932181-202
ISBN 13: 9781932181203

Book and cover design by Jane Jeszeck/www.jigsawseattle.com
Cover photograph by Rick Rapfogel

Printed in the United States of America

acknowledgments

My primary debt is to the children who were (and continue to be) my teachers: Tuhin, Josh, Jesse, Lucy, Sarah, and my nephews. I thank you, with much love and respect.

Second, I thank the many clients who, over so many years, have engaged me in searching conversations about how to be the best possible parents. Your experimentation with the principles I present in this book have both confirmed and deepened my understanding of positive parenting, and my faith that it is possible.

All the theory on which this book is based derives from a creative and visionary group called Radical Psychiatry. Beginning in the early 1970's, we worked as "lay therapists" to invent an approach to psychology grounded in social theory rather than assumptions of pathology prevailing at the time and re-emerging today. We saw people as oppressed, not sick. We believed distressed souls needed the support of communities, not medical intervention. For many years, I joined with colleagues to design and deliver services based on these premises. Because relationship building was so central to our vision, and because we saw conflict as so often destructive rather than creative, we developed means to resolve conflict constructively. What we learned in the course of the mediation work we did informs this book in detail. My thanks especially to Becky Jenkins and Claude Steiner.

Finally, my own mother's sensibility is laced through this text. Her support at critical moments when my needs conflicted with institutional demands, her intervention when I did unusual things that called down upon me condemnation from our shared community, in short, her belief in my capacity to be who I am: in all these ways she parented the child I was, not the child I was supposed to be. These gifts are the foundation for this book. Right along with her support is that of my partner, Mariah Breeding, who cheers me on every step of the way. Thanks to you both.

contents

introduction:
power-sharing parenting

For years I've promised (or threatened) to write a book about parenting. Yes, I know the genre is over-filled to bursting. Besides, it's hard to improve on Dr. Spock. I raised my own kids with his Baby and Child Care tucked under my arm. One long night in a village in India, pacing back and forth to comfort my four-month old first-born as he coughed with what I guessed must be whooping cough, I survived by reading what the phlegmatic doctor had to say. As I remember it: Don't panic, it's no big deal, just make sure the kid is breathing and let nature take care of the rest.

So if the advice you want is focused on what's going on with your child, read Benjamin Spock, or one of the many more recent manuals for raising kids. The advice I've given to my counseling clients over the years is much more about what's going on with them. Children, I believe, grow up; they do what they need to do. Parents, on the other hand, struggle to keep up, often uncertain what they're supposed to do. If the developmental tasks presented to kids are natural, the choices facing parents are largely social in nature.

My son was born in India. I had married into an extended family in a rural area north of Calcutta. I adored my mother-in-law and many of the other older women who lived nearby. Collectively, they had birthed and reared scores of children. Nobody could be more expert.

It had taken me many months to conceive; each time I bled was a time of grief. On one of those days, as faith in my fertility seeped away, I was leaving my house to go to market when the matriarch next door called from her veranda, "When are you due?"

"I'm not pregnant," I replied testily, all too aware that my body had just announced that fact. What a sore spot she'd touched!

"Yes you are," she disagreed. "When your time comes, just call out the window. We'll be there in a flash."

She was right. Despite evidence to the contrary, I'd conceived. Eight-and-a-half months later, Tuhin was born.

So expertise aplenty lived close by. But raising a bi-cultural child quickly taught me something about the nature of expertise.

"Lay the baby down on his back," my neighbors counseled. "He can smother on his stomach."

"Lay the baby down on his stomach," my American mother insisted. "He can choke on his back."

"We'll do his first-rice ceremony at nine months," said my mother-in-law. "Until then, breast milk only."

"I'm shipping you a case of Pablum," wrote my physician father from Texas. "Start him on solids no later than three months; it helps develop his digestive system."

"Dress that baby more warmly!" "What are you trying to do bundling him up like that – smother him?!"

"Let him cry himself to sleep." "The baby's crying; pick him up!"

"Let him sleep in your bed as long as he wants." "He needs to be in his own crib; you don't want to promote dependence, do you?"

The contradictory advice went on and on, each voice as confident as the other. The only thing I knew for sure was that I didn't know a thing. I'd never been very interested in babies until my own was born, and so I'd learned little in advance by observation. Spock was good but a limited vehicle. Much of his advice gently assumed an American, not an Indian, cultural environment. Reading his book, I understood that expertise is highly contextual. Different people deal with very different demands, needs, and cultural frameworks. My father had also sent me crates of diapers and plastic pants; very helpful in a cold urban climate, totally counter-productive, indeed cruel, in the tropics. Whose know-how was I to trust?

Pretty quickly the answer presented itself: the true expert was the baby. Once I got the hang of interpreting his body language and sounds, I discovered I could use an experimental method: If I formulated a hypothesis, he'd present the data. I put him on his stomach and saw how he slept. Then I tried him on his back; he seemed more comfortable that way, but still fidgety. It turned out he was a side-sleeping infant, happiest when curled in a graceful arc on his right side.

My father's baby food arrived. I gave Tuhin a little on a spoon; he spat it out. I waited a week or two and tried again. One day he made a face of disgust and bounced around seeming to be eagerly seeking more. I gave him more. By five months he was reaching for the spoon.

I felt his skin to tell if he was cold and adjusted clothing accordingly. Mosquitoes answered the question about the family bed. Malaria protection aced theoretical risks to his future independence.

By the age of two weeks, Tuhin had taught me my first crucial lesson of parenting:

Childhood is a natural process; parenting is learned activity. Your child is an expert on her or his needs. Observe closely and s/he will tell you what to do, although probably not how to do it.

Simple as it is to state, this premise is fairly stuffed with ideology. It assumes that the nature of children is essentially positive. It runs counter to many philosophies positing in one form or another – original sin or aggressive instincts, for example – that children left to their own devices will be little beasts, that they must be controlled and molded and socialized if they are to grow into virtuous and capable adults.

Beholding the beauty that was (and still is) my son, I didn't know for sure which notion was correct: was he a seed pre-programmed to grow into a glorious oak with only the most essential nutrients, sun, and water provided by me? Or was he a bomb waiting to go off if I weren't alert constantly to defuse him?

I'll write more as we go along about philosophic, religious, cultural, and political underpinnings of different parenting approaches. For myself, all I knew at the time was that I didn't know which view of children's nature was "correct." Once again, conflicting viewpoints confused more than they clarified. But I did know the first alternative—baby as seed—filled me with positive anticipation, while the second raised my dread level intolerably. I'm much happier gardening than policing. So I followed my feelings and very soon discovered that honesty about my ignorance and trust in my baby's capacity to recognize and communicate his needs established a certain power balance in our relationship. From this perception I articulated a second guiding principle:

Cooperation matters: your cooperation with your child. Cooperation is one of those words that can be descriptive or injunctive, depending on whether it's a one-way or two-way street. "Cooperate!" as a command usually means, "Do what I want." It is a corruption of the descriptive meaning: to act together, or to share power.

Children are natural brokers of power. Understandably they, like adults, want as much control over their lives as they can muster. Sharing power to the greatest extent possible makes for successful relationships, and that is as true between grown-ups and kids as among peers, although it is a good deal less obvious what sharing power means across generational divides.

Children have all kinds of powers that adults may not recognize. Recently my brother was exercising his bragging rights as a second-time-around father of an almost-two-year old, Lucy. "Lucy said her first four-word sentence yesterday," he told me proudly when we talked long distance across the continent that separates our families.

"Oh yeah? What did she say?"

"She said, 'Swing push now, Dada.'"

Immediately, I heard from the background Lucy's confident voice: "No no, Dada. 'Swing push more, Dada.'" Not yet two and correcting her father's failing memory! She clearly had power in the sense of capability, many capabilities in fact: to listen, to remember, to recognize a difference between her sentence and his, to speak out at the appropriate moment. She also demonstrated an understanding of her rights: to be understood, to have an independent point of view, and to give voice to her opinion.

That Lucy asserted all those powers was no accident, no quirk of individual temperament. To the greatest extent possible, Lucy's parents make a practice of according her the power of decision making about her own needs. When they visited me in California, we drove to the Pacific coast, Lucy and her mom in the back seat of the car. In the rear view mirror, I could see the baby struggling to stay awake, and we could all hear her beginning to get cranky.

"It would be a pretty good time for a nap," her mom said reasonably. "Would you like to sleep a little while? That way, when we get home in an hour you'll be wide awake and ready to play with the puppy."

Lucy shook her head no and promptly fell asleep.

A clever framing by a perceptive mom who knew just when her kid was about to pass out? Maybe. But it was also establishing a particular kind of dialogue, one in which parents have the power to make wise suggestions based on experience, but kids have the power to determine their own course. Lucy's mom also recognized the limitations of her own power: How do you force a two-year-old in a car seat to take a nap?

Negotiations like this one may be easy in theory, you might protest, but get real! How far will a policy of negotiation take you when you have to get the kid out the door and to childcare on time so you won't get docked a day's pay at work? And if the kid gives me attitude, you ask? Do I have to be "reasonable" or do I get to discipline her?

The practicalities of life do matter, including parents' needs for respite, respect, and relief. When I talk about "power sharing" I really do mean "sharing." Parents have rights, too. My sister-in-law might equally have said, "Lucy, I'm beat. Do me a favor and go to sleep." It may not be obvious how to reconcile adult needs with responsible parenting. That's not easy; not only because of the "laws of parenting" that we all absorb through our pores, but also because of limitations imposed by the conditions of our lives. For the moment, I ask you to trust that my discussion will get down to the nitty-gritty of the "how to" as we go along.

Right now, though, I want to make three arguments for "why to," share power, resting in four different time perspectives.

1) *The present:* Declining the role of control and command allows for a surprising amount of space for fun and love. Grown-ups may be called upon for a bit more forbearance, but children recognize and respond to respect just as the rest of us do. They like adults better. They want to play with us. Sometimes, they even want to be kind to us. It's a really nice way to share family life.

Quite seriously, learning early on how to negotiate differences diminishes those far more disagreeable forms of conflict: temper tantrums (yours as well as your child's), stubbornness, and the myriad of other creative forms of power struggle that both kids and adults use. The family is a microcosm of our diverse society. Kids and grown-ups have different interests, cultures, languages, and styles of conflict. Just as in the big world out there, respecting differences requires some work but pays off in more peaceable and interesting relationships.

2) *The past:* Childrearing, like all human activity, has a history. Like much of human history, it is laced with violence. Corporal punishment is an obvious part of coercive parenting. If authoritarian parenting is your bent (you've probably figured out that it is not mine), then you'd better break a child's will very early in life—which is to say, instill fear of physical harm—or you're likely to find yourself resorting to actual harm right up until the time when the child suddenly realizes s/he has a height advantage over you.

There are different theories about the roots of violence on a societal level—wars, homicide, and so on—in childhood experience. Books have been written giving evidence that vast majorities of convicted murderers were violently abused themselves as children. I believe these linkages contain truth, but I also think that blaming violence in the home for every possible social ill is too simple and places far too much responsibility on parents. All sorts of institutions are coercive and, depending on definitions, violent, from the presence of danger at work to the absence of social supports for people who are ill and in need. At the same time, I believe violence at home is both consequence and at least one thread of cause in the history of violence in the world. The family is a social institution as well as a personal domain. The past is a story of violence running through virtually all human institutions.

Having lived with the fear of punishment, children grow into adults with little faith in alternatives: either punish or be punished. Moreover, coercive parenting teaches children to belie their own wants and perceptions and to place faith in those with greater power. Populations lacking self-determination are unlikely to build societies based in wise and skilled civic participation. Where, after all, do citizens learn those skills?

3) *The future:* The more autonomy a child is allowed in the present, the more responsibility the child will demonstrate later. In other words, a stitch in time saves nine. That's the pragmatic argument for allowing kids as much leeway as possible to make their own choices—including mistaken ones: "Remember how unhappy you were yesterday when you didn't take a nap, Lucy? Might be better to doze a bit now."

I've practiced counseling and mediation in the same community for over thirty years. I've had the rare privilege of working with people when they were eight and now when they are thirty-eight. Some parents whose parents I counseled now come to me with their children. I haven't done a scientific study, but it is my strong impression that little kids who have experienced respect for their rights and powers grow into teenagers who respect the rights of others, including their parents.

They are the easiest of adolescents. Having learned how to exercise power responsibly as two-year-olds (in two-year-old terms), they have no need to seize it crudely later. So much of that dreaded adolescent behavior—what gets labeled "acting out"—is, I believe, an abrupt and inexpert assertion of rights and power that have historically been denied. Kids who have lived those rights and powers right along not only know how to continue in teenage mode but also are more apt to feel the security and confidence to do so with compassion for others. They know how to negotiate—and so do you.

4) *The far future:* Change begins in the places where we can accomplish it. Those of us who are adults today inherited a world of war and injustice. I want to bequeath to my grandchildren something very different. Humans clearly have the capacity to do some vicious things to each other. I deeply believe that we have just as great a capacity to do good as well as a clear inclination in that direction given half a chance. Indeed, I think it takes a lot of doing to corrupt love and turn it into violence and hate. If I aim to parent in ways that allow my kids to be the best people they can be, then I'm doing what I can to introduce them to a world of justice. I want my family to be a microcosm of the world I wish we all inhabited, and that means that I, as a parent, need to be attentive to the ways I use my power and to the justice of my actions.

A belief in goodness is fundamental to my approach to relationships between adults and children. I appreciate that others may feel morally bound to emphasize discipline and control as responsible parenting and that those directions proceed from a belief that there is something inherent in children that needs to be disciplined and controlled.

There is an alternative basis for authoritarian parenting: that children need to learn self-control in order to negotiate a world that is out of control. The more oppression people experience as a group—those subject to racism or classism—the more urgency they may feel to protect their children by controlling them.

So is it possible to parent in an injurious world without doing injury to our own loved ones? Can parents raise children justly in an unjust world? To predict "badness" in children is, in my experience, to elicit it. A form of that same principle operates about other people: seeing the world divided into good and bad leaves one with little recourse but to expect the worst from others—also not a stance that is likely to help children develop good judgment about other people's trustworthiness. If I believe not in a purely beneficent world out there but in my own goodness along with my children's, then the next step is also to believe in my power to elicit the best from my kids through my good example and my persuasiveness. And "the best" includes knowing how to negotiate a less-than-kindly world out there.

All of which is fine and good in theory, but how does one implement such high-flying principles in practice? The lives of most parents are over-crammed with busy-ness. Full time work, if one is lucky enough to have it as opposed to a maddening series of part-time jobs, leaves little time or energy for patient negotiation with a two- or a fifteen-year-old. For all the labor-saving devices of modern life, a typical parenting day in America involves an average of somewhere around six hours of domestic work (still unevenly divided, by the way, between men and women)—laundry, shopping, cooking, cleaning, bookkeeping, helping with homework, and schlepping children from one place to another—in addition to at least eight hours (more commonly these days ten to twelve hours) of paid labor, in addition to an hour or two or more of commuting. Add up those figures and you get sleep-deprived, stressed, irritable, depressed, and anxious parents trying to do the best they can to raise children according to the advice of "experts" like me: not a pretty picture. That workload also adds up to isolation. Where is the time to visit with friends, to organize cooperative childcare, or to help a neighbor clean a house that's gotten beyond her control?

This beings me to my third guiding principle of parenting:

It takes a village to keep a parent functional. Isolation is a parent's greatest peril. Yet it is built into the structure of today's family life. Not only do parents have too little help, but they also lack the emotional support, the encouragement, reassurance, and old-fashioned love needed to sustain them in one of the hardest tasks any of us does: raising kids. Then too, children are isolated as well, and the consequences make parents' jobs harder. Kids may have friends at school, but few children can access those friends after school hours without transportation help from an adult, and school itself is often so structured that kids have too little opportunity to build their own relationships with peers. Nor do children have much chance to experience positive relationships with a variety of adults. Extended kin often live at some distance and their friends' parents are often as busy as you are. All these deficits show up in terms of youngsters' unfulfilled needs being brought home to their own families. They show up, for instance, as competitiveness with siblings for parental attention. I'm not aware that anyone has researched how many hours of parents' time goes into mediating fights among siblings, but I'm willing to bet it's a lot. If much of that friction is not innate "sibling rivalry" but instead a healthy competitiveness for a scarce resource, attention, and support, then options open up for doing something about it. But the obvious things to do bump squarely up against the isolation of nuclear families and the structure of working lives.

So here's what I'm NOT going to do in this book. I'm not going to tell you that this or that or the other is the right way to parent and you are inadequate for not doing it. I'm very aware of the privilege I had beginning to raise my son in an extended family surrounded by an elaborate community. Although that particular family didn't last long into my career as a parent, the experience challenged all the models of family and of motherhood I'd encountered before. Later, I sought out another version in the U.S., an elaborate chosen family surrounded by community.

Drawing on my experience of alternatives, I am going to suggest another way to think about parenting, another vision of relationships and responsibilities and powers within the family, with a full understanding that doing things that way is idealistic because it flies in the face of some very fundamental facts of social life. I'm then going to explore ways of challenging those conditions, which are different for people of different communities, classes, cultures. In other words, my approach is about learning new ways to parent and strategizing new ways to organize life, creating new social conditions, in order to make those ways of parenting possible. Whatever doubts I might have had about how realistic that latter proposition might be, they have been allayed over the years by my clients, the many families who have asked for my help in supporting experiments and adventures in community-based child-rearing.

In the "learning new ways" category, power-sharing parenting involves resistance to many of the moral injunctions that influence parents, taking a critical look at the "shoulds" and "supposed-tos" that inhabit the moral ether around families. It also involves growing skills in negotiation, emotional literacy, expressiveness, and reason.

The "creating new social conditions" category involves building community, rethinking the definition of family, renegotiating divisions of labor, and critically evaluating the function of particular kinds of labor.

To parent in a power-sharing way, in other words, is to sign on for a role as social activist as well. Another burden, you think? Yes and no. There is work involved in doing the things I'm talking about, but there are also ready rewards in the form of easier and richer lives for both kids and parents.

plan of the book

The book is divided into two parts. Part One lays out a developmental order of things. Stages are defined by the challenges greeting parents at various ages of their kids. To some extent the conceit that this is a book about parents' developmental stages is a fiction; questions about parents can't be separated from questions about kids. Clearly, the questions for parents are posed by their children. But parents are also distinct individuals living lives in multiple and complex worlds. At each stage of the process, I seek to keep a focus both on the tasks of parenting and on the lives of parents.

Part Two looks at a number of issues. Some of these will have appeared in the age-appropriate chapters. But many of them, such as discipline or dealing with death, may appear at any point along the way. In a series of short chapters, I've tried to focus on some questions that frequently arise in my therapy practice.

Throughout, I've drawn on stories of particular families. Most of the people who appear in these pages (with the exception of my own family and friends who have agreed to be here) are fictionalized. A story may be sparked by reality, but I've disguised details and created variations, both to protect confidentiality and also to include a greater breadth of experience. I've also tried to reflect at least a bit of the diversity of our society. Of necessity, my knowledge of the lives of people from heritages that are distinctly different from my own is drawn from work with clients and from the generous input of friends and colleagues. I don't pretend to have included all possible cultural identities, veering toward those peoples with whom I'm most familiar (there are more people of European and African heritage, for instance, than of others). I fully realize that for many readers greater rather than lesser acts of extrapolation may be necessary. I both apologize for leaving you with that additional work and I welcome your feedback. The richer the sharing of experience available to us all, the better parents we can be and the better world we can make.

part i:
the stages

1

cooperation and communication:
infancy

> Developmental challenges:
> 1) Learning teamwork
> 2) Understanding baby talk

It begins with the notion that we should be ecstatic about new life, and the *shoulds* and *shouldn'ts* of parenting grow steadily more daunting from there. In reality, few events change one's lifestyle so immediately and so dramatically as does the arrival of a child. The meaning of that event, and the emotions a parent may feel about it, vary enormously depending on a family's condition (isolated or extended, older parents or teenagers, adopted child or birthed triplets), culture (valuing large families or small, education or athleticism, emotionally restrained or expressive), and circumstance (rich or poor, renter or owner, settled in one place for generations or peripatetic).

Many of today's parents are full-bore involved in working lives that can be seriously altered by the abrupt introduction of children. Not only may an individual's identity be vested in a career, but also increasingly her (or his) experience of community may be lived far more extensively at work than at home. Infancy therefore often means a new isolation for a parent, or possibly finding yourself suddenly plunged into a new circle of acquaintances. Moreover, people who have mastered job-related skills, who feel competent and appreciated at work, may find themselves juggling a mysterious new creature screaming passionately for no discernable reason, wiggling and turning alarmingly red in the face. It may have been a long, long time since you felt quite so helpless, quite so adrift. If you're lucky, you may have an elder around to help, or a sibling who arrived at these shores a bit ahead of you. Yet even the business of accepting other's expertise may be complicated, triggering uncomfortably competitive dynamics within your family of origin.

On the other hand, you may take to infant care like a pro. Perhaps you handled a string of younger siblings, or you worked your way through college as a nanny. You may be surrounded, as at a point in time I was, by scads of competent moms, all lending a helpful hand with no strings attached – but counseling you to do things in a way dramatically at odds with your pre-parenthood ideas.

Given all that variation, what happens when you believe you are supposed to feel uncomplicated joy? How do you feel when deep down you've bought the idea that parenthood comes naturally, that mother-hood especially should be instinctive?

adrift in a sea of infancy

I gave birth in a hospital (or what people in India call a nursing home) in Calcutta. Despite my neighbor's generous offer of midwifery, I was insecure about delivering without a functional hospital nearby. My ac-culturation to reliance on professionally-defined medical resources was too strong. So, at seven months pregnant, I decamped to the big city 300 miles and full-day's travel away by car and train and boat and train again.

In the end, we almost couldn't get to the hospital; it was monsoon season, the city was underwater, the car's brakes were shot. But we made it, and after several days we brought the baby to the home of the rela-tives with whom we were staying. I'd looked forward to this moment, as much for the rich support I assumed the environment would offer as for anything else. Lilidi was in her sixties, a warm, intelligent woman who'd reared four children and was now actively grandmothering four more. Her husband, Jaimababu, was a physician. He hadn't practiced for years, serving instead as an administrative medical officer for the government. Their eldest daughter and her three kids were staying with them at the time. Another daughter lived nearby with her husband and year-old baby.

But when I got home, I found that Lilidi was ill with a heart problem and confined to bed. Jaimababu focused nervously on his wife, to whom he was devoted. Besides, he knew little about the practical side of infancy and was, in fact, a super-nervous surrogate granddad. The resident daughter, who knew lots about babies, was away; her father-in-law had just had emergency surgery for lung cancer. The maid-servant, a woman who cooked and cleaned for the family, had just quit, unwilling to assume so great a work-load. And there I was, my worst vision come true: a newborn in my arms and no one who knew anything close by to help. True, my husband and newly college-graduated brother were with me, and they were certainly supportive. But combining all our knowledge of infants, we added up to something substantially below zero.

The next day, I woke up to strange sounds. Tuhin's little body was regularly, rhythmically jerking. I swept him up, patted him, offered him my breast. He didn't seem to be in distress, but he refused to nurse and jerked and jerked and jerked.

I was going for Dr. Spock when the younger daughter arrived to meet the new baby. She laughed. "First case of hiccups?," she asked merrily. She put a little sugar on her finger and rubbed it in his mouth. The spasms promptly stopped.

If parenting is supposed to be an inborn ability residing somewhere deep inside each of us, especially if we're female, then I was in a lot of trouble.

Let's start by deleting that idea. Parenting, as I've said, is a learned activity, and much of what we know about it in the beginning we've learned without consciousness, without critical reflection. Ideas seep into our minds from many directions. You probably go to movies, watch TV, listen to popular music, read a magazine from time to time, even if only in the dentist's waiting room. All those products that we define as culture combine with a ton of influences that are cultural in a wider sense to shape your attitudes and feelings and beliefs about parenting. Inevitably, you are dealing with those influences, knowingly or subliminally. A clever person once said, "We don't know who discovered water, but it probably wasn't a fish." Culture is our water, the medium in which we form assumptions andunderstand what our experiences mean. Your own experience of being parented, of course, is a basic social influence. You may find yourself justifying your practices by saying, "I was treated that way and it didn't do me any harm." Or you may take the opposite position: "I was treated that way and the last the thing I want is to do that to my kid." In all likelihood, you sometimes take one of those positions and sometimes the other depending on the question at hand, your sense of control, your powers of inventiveness, the resources available, and the prevailing ideas in your present community.

A very basic idea for many people in the modern industrialized world is that parenting is a project for two people. Single parents are seen as "unfortunate"—or worse, irresponsible—people, usually moms, who have failed for some reason to provide the ideal of a two-parent family. Yet 28% of America's households with children contain one parent. Based on US census data, researchers estimate that more than half of all children born during the 1990s will spend some amount of time with a single parent, usually their mother. Prevalent though it is, single motherhood in today's America is drenched in moral judgment. Women raising children alone are held responsible by that ethereal thing known as the mainstream for poverty, crime, homosexuality, and a host of other so-called "social ills" .

But if parenting by one is "a bad thing", the concept of parenting by fours or sixes or twelves lies wholly outside the realm of consideration.

Indeed, however many adults are involved in raising a family—and I will argue that the number is virtually never one, that more adults than a single primary parent are always involved—the socially prevailing picture of parenting is limited at most to two.

I swore as a child and young woman that I wanted no children. I watched how bound my mother's life was by her role as mom. Her lifestyle suited her well, but my ambitions far exceeded any model I had of female parenting; I vowed I'd escape that trap come what may. But then one day I realized my own feelings had changed. My husband and I were living in a rural part of India, in his extended family, peopled by relatives I adored. Surrounding us were gazillions of children, parents, cousins, relatives and neighbors of all stripes. Suddenly, almost literally from one moment to the next, I was hungry for a child. I was about twenty-five and my vision of life turned 180 degrees. But without my realizing it, my feelings about childrearing had been formed in the context of a suburban nuclear family that couldn't have been more different from the social context in which I now found myself.

I believe the most central developmental task facing new parents is learning to work as part of a team, and the two most essential skills required are listening to others' stories and trusting ones own perceptions. Those two processes may seem to conflict with each other, but in reality they are intimately bound together.

reading the baby

Some babies are easy from the start. Peaceable and predictable, they sleep a lot, feed with no problem, and smile on cue at about eight weeks. They're happy being held by everyone, happy being left in a crib with a colorful mobile floating above them.

Then there was Tuhin. He was a visual baby. From a very early age his eyes focused on lights and fans and anything else that was bright and moved. So he wanted to be held upright where he could see the world, and he wanted to be moved frequently from one place to another. That translated into a lot of pacing for his adults.

He also cried a lot. Once we got our newborn back to the village, my mother-in-law quickly diagnosed the trouble as colic. We experimented with my diet, since I was nursing him, to see if it was something I ate. But his squirmy restlessness didn't abate. My mother-in-law applied Bengali remedies, mostly involving human touch, massage, and heat. That all helped, but it took three months before his digestive capacity kicked in and we weren't dealing with a near-constant belly ache.

Amazingly, Tuhin grew restless and cried whenever I ate. My mother- and sisters-in-law insisted on carrying him to the other end of the house, far away as possible, while I had my meals. "He's used to your digestive cycle," his grandmother opined. "It's natural that he reacts when you eat." Our umbilical cord might be severed, but clearly significant strands were still in place. For the next decades I was to learn how many and varied they were.

From the beginning, the routines and approaches we developed were tailored to this particular baby, as well as to the resources afforded by our particular environment. Tuhin was a wide-awake child. He napped for very short periods of time and sought amusement when awake. Fortunately, there were at least fifteen older children around at most any moment, so amusement was plentiful and I could happily arrange to meet his need. How different life would have been had we been all alone in a city apartment! I could well imagine resenting his alertness, struggling with him to give it up and go to sleep, maybe even coming to believe he was intentionally doing it to me.

Under my more munificent conditions, though, I very early became convinced of a different and fundamental principle: babies don't lie. They don't manipulate or power play in any other form, either. What they do abundantly, though, is express. Whether giving voice to discomfort or curiosity or a desire for human touch or a passion for visual stimulation, Tuhin always told the truth.

My job was to learn his language. Communication involves a sender and a receiver. He sent; could I receive? There is little in life more heartbreaking than tending to a wailing baby when you can't figure out what's the matter. Sometimes you're left with no option but to comfort rather than satisfy. But that's because of a misfire between the infant's language and the grown-up's comprehension or resources.

In my extended family in India, that premise lay beyond question. In the United States, however, I commonly hear people say things like, "Don't give in every time s/he cries, or s/he'll learn s/he can manipulate you. S/he's got to learn s/he doesn't get what s/he wants simply because s/he wants it."

I imagine these sentiments may translate into, "I'm too worn out to respond when s/he cries, and there's no one else here to do it for me." As a problem statement, I understand it, the problem being too much work, too little labor around. But voiced as a moral statement, a declaration of the *right* way to do it, I disagree. On the other hand, if the objective is to raise citizens who don't express their needs, who don't protest, who are willing to suffer silently and alone, then the methodology makes sense.

Bedtime is a case study in how all those themes play out. Establishing sleep patterns is a major concern of parents in America. In rural India, bedtime is a non-concept. Family life continues late into the night. As the women prepare and serve the last meal of the day and the men visit and talk about the day's events, children play until they tire, eventually curling into the available lap of a woman sitting on the floor to cook, or cuddling up beside a man as he smokes and chats in the dim light of a lantern. The grown-ups' last task of the day is to collect the sleeping children and sort them into the appropriate family beds.

Imagine translating that method into an urban industrial setting. In India, the whole family naps in the afternoon. Two or three hours of down time, followed by more work in fields or kitchen or shop in the cooler hours of the evening, make for a relaxed but awake transition to bedtime. An extended household supports many children, who occupy themselves as a group with little need for adult attention. And when they do gravitate toward the very natural human impulse to fall asleep against the warmth of another human body, there are plenty of bodies available.

In your family, however, chances are good that only one or two adults are around for bedtime, and they are likely to be exhausted from a long day on the go without rest. Parents' need for time off clashes sharply with children's need to play out their day. Battles circling around children's bedtime, so frequent right through adolescence, begin now with a decision about whether to let your infant cry her/himself to sleep. The temptation is strong. Not only are you probably sleep deprived, but you may be suffering from the shock of your dramatically altered relationship with time. Before baby, however busy you may have been with work, relationship, domesticity, and friends, you nonetheless had at least small periods of time alone. You rested, or jogged, or thought, or bathed. Now, however, even when the baby naps, you face an endless set of tasks threatening to bury you unless you hurry, hurry, hurry, racing against the alarm of your infant's wake-up cry.

Combined with the practicality of establishing, by any means necessary, an early end to the baby's day, are a set of moral imperatives that justify your taking action. Here's how that story goes: Learning to fall asleep to the clock, doing it alone, without extra comfort or overly-extensive ritual, we are told, is good for the child. It establishes self-reliance. It teaches a healthy realism about expectations of too much nurturing. It ensures that the child gets enough sleep, "enough" being a quantity scientifically established by physicians. It may seem harsh to let your baby cry to the point of exhaustion, but it really is not. It is for the child's benefit, and sometimes parents must put away their own sentiments when a hard thing to do is also the right thing to do. Mother and father know best, especially when they adhere to the norms of what's best as they are widely established in the community.

I can only imagine how horrified my in-laws would have been had I given voice to such an opinion.

Assumptions about the value of inculcating independence in infants often play into decisions about where to put the baby to sleep. In recent years, the notion of the family bed has gained some currency. In village India, of course, any other kind of bed would be seen as totally weird. But in the U.S., it is an innovation. Babies are natural cuddlers. Fresh from the womb, touched during feedings and play, newborns can have little familiarity with the sensation of sleeping alone. I've mentioned that mosquitoes resolved this question for me; I was lucky to be able to experience first hand the ease and comfort for all of us of sharing a bed. How often I hear parents complain that they fall asleep in their children's beds while putting the youngsters to sleep, waking in the night with stiff neck and sore back and having to re-bed themselves.

Now let's rewrite the bedtime story applying a different set of moral principles and skills for listening and power sharing. Start with the premise that you *don't* know best, that your baby is the expert. Next, observe your particular infant's patterns clearly (as clearly as you can given your own sleep deprivation; maybe you need to recruit someone to cover childcare for a couple of hours in the afternoon so you can nap and be clear enough at night to observe?). What are the rhythms of napping? What signs of tiring do you see at night? How does the baby respond to noise and activity in the environment when those signs appear? How about light and dark? Does the child want to nurse or to have a bottle? Does s/he seem more content lying down with someone beside her/him, or does s/he want to be walked and jiggled and serenaded?

Well informed about your individual infant's sensibilities, you need next to register your own. What do *you* need at nighttime? Here's the point at which the social and the biological meet. Your need is probably more dictated by non-natural factors, like how much help you've had during the day, whether you've worked outside the home that day, how many other primary care adults are around at bedtime, what time you have to get up in the morning, whether you have a dishwasher and a washing machine, and a thousand other details about the construction of your life. Given all those conditions, what you need is reasonable and probably pretty compelling. But is it possible?

Possibly not, at least not in a perfect way. The more people involved in childcare, the closer you may be able to come to finding a balance point that best embodies care for everyone, you included. But if you truly believe that your wants and your baby's wants are equally legitimate and that you share equal rights to satisfaction (a concept I'll elaborate later in this chapter), then you are facing a practical dilemma, not a moral one or an issue of parental responsibility to shape and discipline a malleable and willful child. Even at the very beginning of life, implicit judgments are communicated to children. Your job (in my way of thinking about parenting) is to recognize ideas you've learned, indeed that you've so thoroughly internalized as to regard as natural truths rather than debatable ideas, that serve to justify choices involving an imposition of your will on your baby. You may not be able to satisfy the child's desires and needs entirely, but you can protect your offspring from internalizing the idea that s/he is somehow bad for wanting it.

There is, in my view, a distinct reason for reframing necessity as morality. If you think you're a good person for forcing your baby to sleep according to the clock, you are more likely to accept the assignment, as well as to feel relieved from responsibility. But if you think it is the nature of your social world that positions you to do something less ideal than you would like, you're more likely to challenge that world, to join a campaign for increased maternity leave or family time, for instance. Similarly, you may have to exert less physical force to get children to obey if you insist you are acting in their best interest, and on the other side you may have to practice more skills of persuasion, more imaginative compromise, more self-reflection about where you really can compromise, all of which take time and energy.

Translating the principle of negotiation into practice may take different forms depending on your family structure and circumstance. If you are alone at night with a baby, and if you need to get up in the morning to, let's say, drive a school bus (meaning that the lives of other children depend on your being reasonably rested) and if you can't join forces with other adults who share the routines of bedtime that most resemble your baby's style, then you might opt for an evening that is as quiet as possible, that begins bedtime early and allows rituals of cuddling, feeding, singing, story-telling, that are restful both to you and to the baby. That choice might mean that you do less laundry, cook less elaborate meals, tolerate a messier house. In other words, try to make space for bedtime uncrowded by the thousand other tasks of housekeeping that claw at your consciousness.

This last idea is truly complex. There is a fine-grained mixture of necessity, aesthetics, and ingrained social rules embodied in the standards of housekeeping. Over the years of mediating couples, both heterosexual and same sex, I've had demonstrated to me with great vividness how much gender enters into questions of maintaining domestic space. Women typically (although certainly not always) feel compelled to keep the kitchen surfaces well wiped, the laundry up-to-date and neatly folded, the toys put away, and the floor vacuumed, before they can fall exhausted into bed. How often I hear women complain that their male partners fail to share the load, only to have the men complain that when they do try to "help," the women criticize their low standards of cleanliness:

"I don't mind washing the dishes, but I get really mad when she takes them right out of the dish drain and washes them again!"

"You call that dish washing?! I call it a rinse, and just barely that!"

Environmental aesthetics matter deeply. Many women tell me they need their physical space to be orderly before they can claim consciousness as their own. Men, in contrast, more commonly say, "I want to read the paper, check my email, make love, paint the garage....and then I'll clean up the room." Market researchers maintain that women's brains are made for multi-tasking, while men need to focus on things serially, first one task, then another. And while they are doing each one, they have the power to exclude from their peripheral vision anything extraneous.

I'm not convinced this difference is altogether biological. Biology, I consider, presents us with continua, ranges of capacities and possibilities. From girlhood, the kinds of things women are stereotypically trained to do—talking with friends, dressing elaborately, playing at family life—require holistic thinking, broadly encompassing perceptions of things spoken, seen, sensed, remembered, known, and surmised. Even in today's less-gendered world, girls' toys elicit a variety of imaginative interactions. Boys, though, are trained to focus on a ball or a computer, on one thing at a time. Action figures come with more distinct story lines, and even video games compel awareness to a screen and a repetitive action.

For women, then, a chaotic environment may be disquieting, while for men it may be simply a task postponed. That working women often crowd their evenings with housekeeping reflects both wide-ranging capabilities and internalized oppression. When I wrote my first book, I realized some segment of my crowded life would have to go. I wouldn't give up full-time parenting; I had to continue earning money. I looked around the house, gulped, and made a vow to pick things up only after each draft was done. It seemed clear that those were my choices: a neat house or a completed book. It was a hard thing, not a relief, to let go of the housework, but it was that or suppress my writer's voice.

Ideally, if you are co-parenting with a partner, your bedtime choices are broader than I've suggested. You might negotiate with that person to share bedtime in a variety of ways, seeking the ones that best serve everyone's purposes. You could alternate nights, or trade bedtime for a morning shift, if you have an earlier start time than your partner has. Finding that the baby responds well to having you both present, you might do the rituals together, hoping the time also serves your need for connection with each other. Use your imagination and all your negotiating skills to experiment with variations on the theme, noting and selecting the most effective ones. And just as you get the routine down, be prepared to notice that your infant's patterns are changing. They change constantly as the baby grows and discovers new capabilities, including a growing appetite for wakefulness.

Throughout all of that, practice saying to yourself and to your baby that the problem is not that s/he wants too much or is too dependant or demanding or needy. The problem is that you're simply not in a position to respond perfectly, and (practicing for the emotional complexity of your baby's next stage, the "terrible twos") that you feel sad, or angry, or whatever it is you do feel about the situation. You might also try practicing optimism: The longer you learn parenting together, the better you'll work the problems out.

how to work cooperatively

The approach I'm suggesting for handling bedtime is also good training for learning to negotiate, both with your child and with your co-caretakers. For the lucky few of you who live with more than two adults, the negotiation of needs becomes easier, and also more complex, a small price to pay for the extra help. If the baby speaks the truth, then the problem becomes building enough help into the baby-care system so that parents can afford to listen.

Let's start with an inventory of your "team." Who are the adults involved in childcare? Do you have a spouse? A partner? A grandparent or several? A neighbor? A friend? A paid caretaker? Hopefully, you have some number of people laying hands on the baby in a regular and helpful way. Some friends, a straight couple, gave birth to their firstborn, Jesse, while living in a household with two very close single women friends. All four adults were thrilled with the infant, and all four vowed to share parental duties. We learned that the averages were just about right: four adults to one infant. That's the break-even point—the amount of labor needed so that no one individual feels exhaustedly overloaded. True, everyone in Jesse's household worked hard. But the labor-to-baby equation worked well enough.

To construct cooperative working relationships among the adults involved is easy to say, not so easy to do. In fact, most of the ways that many of us are taught in this society to relate to others are the opposite of cooperative. We're taught to fight for what we want, to view others as adversaries, to compete to win. Exceptions to that pattern often exist in families newly immigrated from more communal societies. But as the generations go on, individualism, and with it competitiveness, tend to crowd out those cultures of origin.

What lies on the other side of individualism is, paradoxically, self-sacrifice. If we're not competing, then we're likely to be caretaking. Messages abound about putting others before yourself. To be selfless is to be noble. Especially in family relations, we are taught that "compromise" is inevitable, that you can't get your way all the time, that accepting loss and restriction equals maturity, concepts that begin at birth and continue throughout.

Both sides of the coin—coercion and self-sacrifice—can only operate under conditions of dishonesty. That's a harsh word to use for the many little lies we tell ourselves and others, born of contradictions between integrity and what we don't know how to do. Mom may, for instance, feel ashamed of her inability to be endlessly patient with a cranky baby and her inability to be endlessly forgiving of a less-than-helpful mate. So she may say she's doing fine and doesn't need help, right up until the moment when she explodes in anger. Or she may nag and needle rather than admit she's incapable of further activity and deeply in need of relief. Self-sacrifice and coercion take turns with each other, an endless swing from sweetness to tyranny.

Meanwhile, her partner may look away from signs of her impending collapse, justifying inattention by his conviction that he brings home more money and (in his most private thoughts) doesn't a greater income make him a more worthy person? Or at least more worthy of peace and quiet at the end of the day? The notion may jostle uncomfortably with sympathy for the woman he loves as she goes down for the third time and resentment over her fastidiousness and volatility. But none of this does he say out loud, hiding instead in front of the eleven o'clock news.

Both partners are, on an emotional level, living with secrets and lies of a sort that come home to roost, usually in the form of battles at the breakfast table, if not earlier in bed.

All these behaviors are strategies for handling problems, and, especially in combination, they produce disunity and contention. Cooperation begins with ruling the behaviors out:

- **No power plays** (any act intended to get another person to do what she or he wouldn't otherwise do)
- **No self-sacrifice** (any act intended unilaterally to assume a disproportionate or untenable amount of the work)
- **No secrets or lies** (any act intended to manage relevant information, of an emotional or a factual nature, by withholding it)

Simple rules, but don't try them while driving! Taken together, they describe an open, collaborative, mindful, and, above all, reciprocal relationship. If you are abiding by these three injunctions, what you are left with is honest discussion, creative resourcefulness, shared problem-solving, and good-willed negotiation. Clearly, those practices are better accomplished with some people than others. Specifically, cooperative relationships call for a measure of equality, if not perfect equality of power, then at least a very firmly entrenched equality of rights.

There are plenty of times when power plays and secrets are exactly in order. You may not want to tell your boss just what you think of him or you may want to construct a careful strategy to add political muscle to your attempt to take control of the school board. When you find yourself in a truly adversarial position with people who are not about to let their guard down, don't try to act cooperatively; one hand can't clap and if you try, you may be surprised to find your hand smashing painfully against the wall. Times when you have less real power than the person or people in contention with you—a boss, or a business competitor, or someone of a more privileged social identity, there may be justification for power playing by withholding information, or even sometimes lying. Of course, there is an ethical dilemma each of us faces in these circumstances. There is an injury incurred to the integrity of the person who chooses to act less than honestly, less than cooperatively, under whatever circumstances. I would wish for a world in which negotiation in good faith were the prevailing norm. But in the real world, often it is not. Unequal and uncooperative relationships are unfortunately common, and the consequences if one person acts openly and honestly while another does not, especially if that person is more powerful, can be severe.

So the guidelines for cooperation I'm suggesting are only useful when everyone involved is equally committed to them, and when the capacity for each person to negotiate for her or himself at least approximates equality. "Equality" is a complex matter; between children and adults, for instance, where does equality lie? I make a distinction between mechanical equality and a commitment to equal rights. The starting place for cooperative relationships is the assumption that no one is more entitled to getting her or his needs met or interests satisfied than anyone else. How exactly you manage that is not always obvious, but the principle needs to be profoundly adopted for the question to become meaningful.

In this context, then, what's the problem with self-sacrifice? As I've commented, many cultures honor it. Its opposite is construed to be selfishness, an accusation most acutely leveled at girls and women who are, according to traditional rules of gender, enjoined to nurture relationships by putting others' needs before their own. Indeed, particular individuals are enjoined to endure different sorts of sacrifices: men, perhaps, to be good providers at any cost to self; women to "do it all" with successful careers, perfect housekeeping, and all-patient partnering and parenting. In the process, we burn out, get grumpy, or lose heart—all sorts of nasty consequences that are the mirror opposite of those intended.

At the same time, in a competitive economy there is a counter-injunction—to compete hard and win, to put oneself before others at all cost. We're taught those rules through sports and academic rankings. These contradictory messages all assume a dualism: that self-sacrifice and selfishness are two opposite and self-canceling qualities. When it comes to parenting, I'm suggesting they take on very different meanings. It is neither selfish nor selfless to speak up for your own needs while simultaneously respecting everyone else's, because both sides of that equation hold information crucial to finding solutions that truly work for everyone and therefore stand the test of time.

negotiating solutions

Let's go back to baby's bedtime and play out scenarios in which no one either power plays or sacrifices. Right away, you might protest, there is a critical contradiction: self-sacrifice is not an infant's problem; small children are hardly known to be willing negotiators. They insist on what they want with little regard for the well-being of their caretakers.

True, and also not true in some important ways that I'll talk about as they come up. For the moment, however, I'm focusing more on transactions among those whose equality is more obvious, the caretakers. Because I believe it is isolation, so common among parents in nuclear families, that gives rise to so many of the problems we take to be inherent to child-rearing, I prioritize the mindset, and with it the skills, that best increase chances for as much labor sharing as possible.

In two-parent families, negotiating bedtime duties is often thorny. At the end of long, grueling days, most of us are not at our most co-operative best. Whatever store of extra energy for talking through a problem there might have been in the morning is now long gone. So one good strategy is to have the conversation about bedtime at some time other than bedtime.

Start with each person speaking fully about her or his experience of the occasion.

Parent One: "Working part-time, I'm home earlier than you. So I pick Sally up from childcare, do the grocery shopping, come home and start dinner. All that while the baby is cranky because she's been away all day. I'm trying to entertain her and comfort her, which means I'm juggling her on one arm while I'm lifting grocery bags with the other. By the time we're ready to put Sally to bed, I'm done. I'm not up for the process."

Parent Two: "I know you do all that, and I so appreciate it! Here's my dilemma: Working a full-time job while trying to be a responsible co-parent has me exhausted. I'm sure I'm not more tired than you, but I am tired. I've been dealing with dissatisfied customers all day, glued to a computer screen. All I can think of is a shower and bed."

It's so much about scarcity. Where are the grandparents and aunts and uncles? Where are the neighbors who are themselves raising children and who, needing the same things, might band together with you? A place to start is with the possibility of bringing more people into the picture. Can you afford to hire a mother's helper in the evening hours? What a relief it would be to hire a teenager who's willing to entertain Sally while dinner prep is underway, especially if that person could put on a load of laundry, run to the store for forgotten items, and do other small tasks around the house. How about some sharing with neighbors?

Soon after I returned to the U.S. from India, I joined with friends to live collectively. One step along the way to that rather dramatic act was to form community in a neighborly way. We commonly traded off watching the kids and cooking. In fact, it was partly the tedium of carrying pots and pans and sleeping babies from one house to another that encouraged us to live under one roof. I know of four families who have formed a childcare co-op, sharing much of the work in imaginative ways. They talk about the relief, and also about the enrichment of their family lives.

If finances or the absence of teenagers or other parents of young children in the community make these approaches impractical, how can you manage to make the most of what you do have? If you can't bring more working hands into the equation, are there ways to reduce the workload? Re-examine all the chores you do before the baby's bedtime: can you pare them down to the minimum? Are there any of those activities you might "outsource"—buying healthy prepared food to minimize cooking, using paper plates to minimize dishwashing, packing away knick-knacks for the time being to minimize dusting, and so on?

Now we're down to sharing the work out between you both. Start with the recognition that everyone's life is hard right now, that arguing about who has it worse and most deserves relief at bedtime will only get you into another energy-sapping cul-de-sac. A handy technique is to list all the things that need to happen between the end of the working day and the grown ups' bedtime. Next comes the "no self-sacrifice" part, or at least as little as you can manage. First say exactly what you'd want:

Parent Two: "I'd like to disappear into the shower and a rest when I get home. But then I'd really *like* to put Sally to bed. I love lying down with her, cuddling and singing her lullabies."

Parent One: "Well, I really need some down time myself before starting to get the house in order. I'd love dinner to magically appear. If I didn't have to cook, I'd be happy to entertain Sally before she's ready to go to sleep."

Some solutions start to appear. Parent Two might offer to bring dinner home several nights a week, freeing Parent One to play while Parent Two transitions out of the working day. Parent Two might offer to take on bedtime rituals on working days, in return for Parent One compensating with other tasks.

At this point, you're likely to remember all the other items on the must-do list that this draft of a plan doesn't address. Scan the list and speak for the chores you least mind doing. Maybe you can stand taking out garbage but absolutely loath dish-washing. Maybe folding laundry has a certain meditational value, while washing lettuce drives you bonkers. Having both picked your "can-do" items, you'll be left with some things, hopefully only a few, that nobody wants to do. If you can't find someone else to do them, and you can't figure out a way to ditch them, then at least you can divvy them up with a sense of equality. You can also agree to reshuffle the deck when either of you reaches a point of total burnout.

Laced through this model negotiation is the principle of honesty. In fact, I often believe that an agreement to withhold no information—nothing relevant to what's going on between you, that is—and to tell no lies covers the entire subject of cooperative negotiation. If you are speaking up for what you want and feel, you've laid down the crucial basis for working through solutions that are most cooperative and most likely to work.

The steps are:

- *Say exactly what you want.* If you start out compromising, by the time you negotiate more compromises you'll end up with an agreement you can't stand to implement. By asking for 100% of what you want (but no more; don't "position" yourself for a negotiating edge against a loved one), you stand a much better chance of coming up with an agreeable agreement.

- *Listen to your negotiation partner's "100%" and believe it.*

- *Work together to seek ideal solutions, ones that give you exactly what you want, or even maybe something more than either of you imagined. (I found collective living to be in the latter category.)*

- *Having exhausted those possibilities, look for compromises that do least injustice to your sensibilities. Again, if you compromise too much, you won't be able to stay true to your solution. It will fall apart, and you'll have to do it all over again.*

- *Promise to continue to be honest about how your plan is working for you and to renegotiate whenever either of you feels overburdened.* That is a state, by the way, that is often signaled by a sense of grievance against the other partner. Avoid feeling that he or she is taking advantage of you or getting off easy: those ideas hark back to adversarial relationships, not to what you've both (hopefully!) signed on for. Give your partner the benefit of the doubt, but pay attention to those feelings of resentment, reading them as signs that your system needs revision. Speak up rather than unilaterally rewriting the agreement.

making even harder decisions cooperatively

Resolving workload issues cooperatively is one thing. Making those many difficult, culturally charged decisions that accompany infant care may be another. There are choices that carry intense religious significance, for instance. Circumcision is one of those. Heavily grounded in cultural traditions, the circumcision of boy infants challenges new parents to sort out their own values and beliefs, and to reconcile them with each other's and with their extended families. Circumcision may identify a boy as a member of a particular identity group, as Muslim or Jewish, for instance. Or it may simply signify compliance with current medical opinion. Recent research questioned the notion that circumcision is a requirement for good hygiene later in life, demonstrating that "science", too, can be thought of as a cultural group.

The family bed is another of those decisions often laced with assumptions and values. As I mentioned in an earlier chapter, I opted to keep the baby with me. It was not a choice I made in a theoretical way, in advance of the reality. In fact, we hired a craftsman to build a lovely teak crib for the baby, cannily constructed to convert into a sofa. And a sofa it remained as Tuhin never slept in it. Here again, the wishes of the whole family need to be taken into account. A restless, breast-fed baby may allow parents more sleep time if s/he's in the bed, while a sound sleeper who never stirs all night might not care after falling asleep. One parent might relish the sensuality of that small body in the night, especially if you've had to be away at work all day. If the other parent wants an adult-only sleep space, then it's time to pull out negotiation procedure and seek those acceptable compromises (family bed some nights, the crib others?).

negotiating with baby

I'll deal with the topic of cross-generational negotiation in greater detail as the chapters go on. I am aware of common objections, starting with the idea that adults really do know some things that children don't. Kids and adults are, by definition, not equal and don't have equal experience nor equal access to resources. Many people's objections go on from there to claims about authority and entitlement. Cooperating with kids, some parents fear, will undermine the authority needed to get through day-to-day life tasks, not to mention keeping teens alive later on. All these questions will come up for discussion as we move along the road of parental development.

For now, I want to make one essential point: all children, from infancy on up, are more responsive to others than we adults imagine. At the very beginning, a newborn can be invited to play or to rest, depending on the body language of the adult holding her. An undiapered baby's bowel habits become predictable within a couple of months, and rituals can be constructed so that the baby goes where you want if you agree to follow his or her lead as to when s/he goes. I tended to nurse Tuhin while reading a book; very soon he connected the two, reaching for the breast when I picked up the book. Later, when he could crawl, he'd tell me he wanted to nurse by bringing me the book I'd been reading last time he fed. He had no words yet, but he surely could communicate. If I had finished the book when he wasn't looking, I had to mime reading the last page and picking up the new one in order to move on. We negotiated the rituals.

The capacity of small children to note their world, to adjust to what goes on around them, to experiment with different ways of doing recurring things like nursing and relating and sleeping, is wonderful. Even though a newborn doesn't understand language, I urge new parents to speak about what they're doing and what they want, for two reasons. First, it's never too soon to cultivate the habit of talking matters through with a child. Second, you may not be aware of how much your tone of voice and other non-verbal signals communicate to an infant. Better, I believe, to err on the side of offering information than it is to assume you can tell what registers for a newborn and what doesn't. Here, too, information is power and power sharing is a good way to go.

2

emotional literacy*:
the "terrible twos"

Developmental challenges:
1) Embracing passion
2) Understanding power

One of my mother's favorite sayings is "This too shall pass!". How often
I've heard parents of two-year-olds express that sentiment in one form
or another. The "terrible twos" are often a stage when tempers fray on
all sides, a time characterized by parents' heavy-duty attempts to tame
their wild offspring, and just as heavy attempts by toddlers to assert
their wills. Few civil wars better exemplify the dynamics of intractable
power struggle. Now is the first real time that a power-sharing approach to parenting can be put to the test.

But it is more than a test; it is the real deal. At two (and often earlier
if babies have been treated the way I suggest from the beginning), the
lines are being established for a lifetime relationship. This is the stage
during which the stage is set for adolescence, and for everything that
comes before and after. I often encourage people to hang in there for
the two-year-old roller coaster with the promise that adolescence will
be a whole lot easier if they take the harder path of sharing power
now.

The means for negotiating power are limited only by human cre-

* a phrase coined by Claude Steiner to suggest that emotional expression, like reading,
is something that must and can be learned.

ativity. Whether engaged in subterfuge, manipulation, coercion, or negotiation, we all have a vast tool kit of behaviors to draw on. We may
bend the truth, or we may stand tall and ball our fists. In a meeting, we
can seize the floor and rail against a proposal. Or we can volunteer to
keep the official minutes and simply fail to write anything until a decision goes our way.

Passion is a profound means for influencing outcomes and the one
that is most accessible to very young children. The expression of strong
feeling has a capacity to move others. Often the person whose intensity
of purpose is most vividly expressed has the advantage, at least for the
moment. Passion reads differently and has different consequences in
different cultural contexts, however. I remember many years ago when
I visited Russia for the first time. Everywhere I went, people screamed
at each other, in person, over telephones, across desks. I was a journal-
ist trying to negotiate permission to visit someplace inaccessible and
I was intimidated by all that emotion, which I read as anger. Gradually, though, I noticed two things: I was not hearing angry screaming in the streets. In America, I was used to random outbursts of fury
among strangers in public settings—road rage, angry mumblings at the
gas pump, eruptions of condemnation toward a panhandler. Yet there in
Russia, all of the transactions were among people in the course of some
kind of ordinary business. And the second thing I noticed was that this
anger, if that's what it really was, was fleeting. After an outburst, people's
tone would return to what I thought of as "normal." Often, there was
a chuckle, a friendly tilt of a chin, a sentence in which I (understanding
no Russian) thought I heard amicable agreement.

For these Russians, expression of anger was the norm, a way of being in relationship with each other that held no threat and signified no
breach.

Think of your two-year-old as Russian. (Of course, if you are Russian, you may want to pick a different metaphor. Or you might want to
write me a letter letting me know how far off my interpretation of Rus-

sian emotional culture really is.) Your child is using a newfound form of activity to express some newly-experienced forms of feeling. But if the society around her or him is emotion-hostile, as I believe mainstream society in America mostly to be, then for the adults around the toddler a temper tantrum carries a whole different set of meanings.

public censure and silent shame

I was at the grocery store recently, waiting in line to check out. A woman with a baby was finishing up before me. The child, about the age that I'm describing, sat in the grocery cart serenely licking a Popsicle. Mom finished her business and moved on, pushing baby and bags before her. As the teenaged "package girl" busied herself with starting to bag my purchases, she shook her head from side to side and chuckled quietly to herself. As soon as mother and child were out of earshot, the young woman burst into speech. Undeterred by my presence, she addressed herself to the checker with disdainful energy:

"You should have heard those two in the ice cream section!" she declared, her voice molting disapproval. "The kid was grabbing everything in sight. Every time the mother opened the freezer door, the baby was practically falling out of the cart grabbing ice cream; the mom was tearing things out of her hands and the kid was screaming at the top of her lungs.

"It was a wreck! Totally out of control! The mother finally gave in and let her have the Popsicle!"

Control was, indeed, the issue, the premise of this young woman's observation being that one of them was in control and one of them was not and that it was the wrong way around. Surrounding that drama, I thought, was another of equal import, this one a contest for social control with its protagonist the clerk and its object the mother. Though this parent was no doubt fastened on the battle with her two-year-old, I'm betting that she was also every bit as aware of the negative gaze of the clerk and that those messages the clerk sent out influenced the mother's actions. Two injunctions tend to be communicated by the onlookers to a parent-child confrontation: first, parents should be able to control their children, and, second, screaming in public is not all right.

Now, I'm aware that a long-screaming child can be irritating. In fact, that part of the equation is something positive, a piece of what might enter into the parent's transaction with the child. The grocery store is prolific in offering "teachable moments." It's one thing to say to a child, "Stop screaming! Everyone is looking at you!" It's quite another to suggest, "Look around you; that person over there is unhappy that you're screaming. Can you maybe lower your volume so we can talk but she's not so bothered?" The suggestion may go nowhere in the moment of passion. But what you're introducing is the idea that the toddler can control her behavior, both by your implication and by the act of proposing to the child an alternative action s/he might take. You're also teaching him/her to notice that s/he has an effect on those around him/her, that s/he is, in fact, a powerful presence.

What the mom-in-the-freezer-section acted out instead were the twin notions that two-year-olds are out of control—that is to say that they have no power of choice over their behavior—and that the parent's job is to exercise control for (or over) the child. The clerk's gaze (even though, based on her mode at the check-out stand, I'd guess the clerk never looked directly at the confrontation but kept her eyes steadfastly averted) communicated the judgment that the mom was weak, the child unruly, and that the relationship as well as the freezer was a "wreck." And regardless of whether the clerk actually felt all of that as clearly or as strongly, it is the sort of situation that constitutes social control both of parental responsibility and of emotional expression.

A big leap? Consider this question: how do you yourself feel about emoting in public? About emotion at all? Do you judge yourself harshly when you "lose your temper"? Think about the language: it suggests that temper is something you are supposed to keep, not lose. The clerk kept *her* temper, even though I considered sympathetically that she might well be really ticked off about having to re-order the freezer. Her anger, I suspect, turned to judgment.

How you emote may well say something about your culture and identity. If you are of northern European heritage, you may have inherited harsher sentiments about anger than if you are of southern European heritage. You may, indeed, never "lose it," although you may wonder whether your inability to be "hot" has something to do with the frequency with which your passionate attachments to other people "cool off," often in fact disappearing into a "cold" heart. If you are African American, on the other hand, you may claim anger proudly. One legacy of America's racial past is the understanding that it was not just bodies that were owned during slavery but emotions, too. Expressions of anger were dangerous, and suppression was acted out corporally as well as through the threat of being forcibly separated from family and community, "sold down the river." Enslaved people learned to manage their protest, to express it in ways that were at least a little safer. Strategies survived into the post-slavery days of Jim Crow. I've interviewed African American people in the south about their experiences of segregation, and they universally told stories of dealing with injustice through humor, private ridicule, and small instances of retribution; the son of a fair-skinned mother, for instance, who rippled with righteous laughter as he recounted how Mama pointedly seated herself in the front of the bus, and only she and he knew the truth. When overt protest was at last unleashed during the civil rights movement, some black Americans determined never to suppress their anger, or any other emotion, again, it gave birth to a cultural stereotype of the angry African American. (Like most stereotypes, this one could not be further from the truth that I've found in my warm, complex, welcoming experiences with people.)

Particular emotional cultures are inculcated early in life, some of them reflecting social communities, others familial traditions. A parent can try to quiet a child screaming in the grocery store in a number of ways, and each one teaches another set of attitudes toward emotion.

Notice how you react to a two-year-old's temper tantrum and think back to how your own outbursts were handled. Were you spanked? Ignored? Fussed over? Did you simply watch an older sibling's struggles with your parents and decide early on to lay low? Or to fight even harder? In my family, anger was seen as a fault. Strength of character was equated with emotional control. My mother often expressed irritation, usually indirectly, in a complaining sort of way. My father's facial expression sometimes suggested his displeasure, but he rarely acted on it. Instead, he was absent a lot, busy with his professional life. When he did interact with us kids, though, his preference was to do it through play and laughter. I got the message that the more powerful parent was silent in the face of anger, engaged when I was smiling, gone when I was not. My choices were laid out before me very early on.

inadvertent lessons

If you have a hard time allowing yourself to be angry, you may communicate to your child the idea that anger is wrong. If you righteously defend your own anger but are worn out by your baby's, you might simply overpower her expression by raising your own voice in a threatening way. In the first case, you imply that anger itself is bad, in the second that annoying you is the problem, not anger in general. Neither one is ideal, but the difference may be a piece in the perpetuation of emotional traditions.

During lunch with a friend in a neighborhood café, a tired-looking mom seated herself at the counter beside her maybe-three-year-old daughter. The mom was juggling the child onto the high stool along with a bottle of juice, a couple of paper cups, and a sandwich. The child immediately reached for a cup and asked for some juice in it so she could drink from the glass by herself (a new achievement, I imagined, of which she was justifiably proud).

The mom, distracted, was simply not fast enough to comply. She said nothing, just continued organizing lunch on the counter, making several trips to a sidebar to collect silverware and napkins. The little girl started to complain, repeating over and over in a voice of rising volume and indignation, "Wanna drink juice from a cup!" The mom ignored her until the decibels reached a certain level and the child was crying as well, and then the mom said:

"We can't cry in a restaurant."

The child paused for a beat. I thought she was considering the contradictions in this statement, since here she was, clearly crying in a restaurant. She then began again, "Juice in a cup!"

"If you keep that up, we'll have to go home," said the mother, looking worriedly around her.

"No, no. Just gimme juice in a cup!"

Without another word, the mother abruptly wrapped the sandwich up in a napkin, closed the bottle of juice, packed them both in her backpack, hoisted the child and carried her screaming out of the restaurant.

In her first response, "You can't cry in a restaurant," the mother communicated a moral lesson: crying in public is not allowed, it is a bad thing to do. And if it's a bad thing in public, then by implication all crying is bad. Perhaps the daughter also heard, "You are a bad child for doing it."

Moreover, the child might have figured out, or would likely figure out some time soon, that in fact not *all* crying is bad. Had she fallen off the high stool and cried in pain and fear, her mother would most likely have cuddled and comforted her. So it is *angry* crying in public that's bad.

The girl made a choice, though, to continue doing the bad thing. Whereupon her mother acted angrily to remove her. The mother didn't cry, however; she made no sound and did nothing verbal. Nonetheless, anger fairly screamed from her every gesture.

Attitudes toward anger can, of course, be contradictory: Do what I say, not what I do. If you want your child to stop having temper tantrums, it may be wise to stop having them yourself. On the other hand, there is a debate among some African-American parents about putting down children's insubordination hard, lest they forget themselves out in a dangerous world and "sass" the wrong person. "Our boys are getting shot out there every day," said one mother, braided fear and anger in her voice. "He's got to learn to sit on his feelings when he's stopped by a cop. How's he going to do that if I let him fly off the handle at home?!"

Other black parents I know argue the opposite side of the coin: How's the child to learn to recognize what he feels and to develop the skills to choose a safe means of expression if he's not allowed to practice at home? Indeed, if the model before him is of a parent caught in her or his own emotions, and using them to suppress and control the child, then isn't the youngster likely to draw exactly the wrong conclusion?

My own son is a young man of color; he, too, has had his terrifying encounters with authority, although I am very aware that he grew up in a relatively protected environment, in a multiracial, middle-class community. I acted to help him name and talk about his feelings in the hope that he could learn to anticipate the reaction he was likely to get, and to modulate his expression accordingly. I must admit, though, that whatever my intention, I had a lot of on-the-job learning to do.

In the beginning, when my son erupted in anger, I tended to work very hard to calm him. I saw him as uncomfortably troubled and I thought it was my duty to solace him and remove the discomfort. I'd try distraction. I'd intervene to fix whatever had triggered his ire. At one stage he was determined to exercise his will on inanimate objects. I think he may have gotten the idea that such a thing was possible because he'd been given a bunch of pop-up books; they moved, things appearing and disappearing in response to the text that I would read him. If the books could move, then he wanted to make them move on his command as well. He'd notice the colorful volumes lying around the floor and say sternly, "Books! Get on the table!" I'd scurry to put them on the table. He'd fly into a rage. "No, no!" he'd insist. "Not you!

On the table, by themselves."

Months later when we were visiting the U.S. from India we em-barked on a cross-country drive with my brother and sister-in-law. There we were in a Volkswagen van with two large dogs, three adults, and my two-year-old son, hour after hour after hour. Under the cir-cumstances I figured tantrums would be inevitable, and I gritted my teeth in anticipation of the first one. When it came (I can't remember the cause), I quickly set out to intervene. But before I could, my sister-in-law began to cheer. "Go, Tuhin!" she said, and then turning to me, "Don't you wish you could do that? What a great tantrum!"

It blew my mind, opening up a whole new attitude toward Tuhin's passions. Do you mean I could relinquish my sense of responsibility and just enjoy them? Here was a very different reading both of feeling and of responsibility. I sat back and waited; sure enough, Tuhin noticed his aunt's grin and started to giggle with her. Bellows and guffaws mixed together, until the storm was past and the van sunny again.

I learned new principles that day; first that emotion, anger includ-ed, is healthy and neither a character flaw nor intrinsically dangerous. Danger comes not from rage but from oppression. Second, I came to believe that parental responsibility is to support emotion not control it. The experience in that VW van encouraged my inclination to expect Tuhin to learn the difference between safe and dangerous settings and, even more, to learn the skills that would enable him to pitch his tenor accordingly.

negotiating stormy weather

Based on these principles, let's consider alternatives to the scene in the grocery store.

The baby grabs a handful of Popsicles out of the freezer. The parent says, "Do you really want to eat one?" The child nods vigorously. The parent says, "Well, one then. Not all of them." The child shakes her head vigorously and her chin begins to quiver. The parent says, "You might get sick if you ate them all. Have one now and I'll buy some more for later." The child considers for a moment, starts to hand the excess Popsicles back, and then changes her mind. She begins to cry, kicking her heels, saying, "NO! All! I want all right now!"

The parent considers for a moment. (Ideally, passers-by smile indulgently and wink supportively at the parent. In reality, other shoppers and clerks are probably either darting disapproving glances or studiedly looking the other way.) If concern about tummy woes is really the problem, one possibility is to let the child have them all; they'll melt long before s/he actually gets to eat them, although if she does get a bellyache she'll probably have verified a cause and effect connection. But there will be a mess, not to mention the cost of a lot of Popsicles (although weighing the couple of dollars it may cost against the lesson taught is not a bad idea). Let's say the parent concludes that one Popsicle in hand is really all s/he's up for. S/he releases the cart handle, looks calmly at the baby, and says, "Yeah, it's a drag, isn't it?, that you can't have them all. It's so tempting. I get that you're angry. Cry it out for a moment and then let's get on with our shopping." S/he waits a beat or two, standing by patiently. If the anger abates, good and well. Parent returns the excess Popsicles to the freezer or the cart and moves along. If not, though, a moment may come to take the Popsicles out of the child's hand, maybe saying, "I'm putting these in the cart and when you're ready to eat one, you can choose the one you want right now. The rest will be for later." The parent may pat the baby, or simply stroke her head, saying, "I know you're still angry. You work it out while I go on with the shopping."

will and expression: hallmarks of the two-year-old
My alternative scenario is a lot more plausible if encounters like the Popsicle drama occur only rarely. In fact, though, at this stage of life, they tend to be a lot more frequent. Why is that and what challenges do the reasons behind such anger pose for parents?

I believe that the most basic reasons why kids this age are so emotionally fraught have nothing to do with the adversarial battle parents
tend to read into the situation. In other words, kids are not saying "No!"
simply to be contrary. Earlier in life, babies are pretty simple mecha-
nisms. They feel things, both physical and emotional things, and they
react. Adults either respond, relieving the stimulus, or they don't. The
infant is hungry; s/he cries; the parent offers breast or bottle. The four-
month-old recognizes a human face and (we think) feels pleasure; s/he
smiles and the face smiles back. By four months babies are playing with
toes and teething rings, by six months sitting up learning to manipulate
Cheerios and spoons. The relationship between thing (human or inanimate) and action is reasonably direct.

But by twenty months or so, things have become a lot more complex. The child is capably mobile, able to walk around at will. Language
is developing, words for this and that if not whole sentences. The baby's
world has expanded greatly, and with it the options for her/his acting
on it as well. The element of choice is now front and center. I can do
this, or I can do that. I can get dressed and go along with Dad to the
store, or I can refuse to get dressed and stay here playing in my room.
Beyond all the physical actions the child is learning to accomplish, s/he
is also experiencing the new pleasure of having far greater determination over time, or more specifically over the course of her own time.
S/he may not yet have very clear concepts of "now" and "later" or of
"today" and "tomorrow," but she does have a concept of doing this
rather than that now.

So far so good. All this learning and experimentation is proper and
productive. Except for one thing: Dad may need to get to the grocery
store *now* and there may not be anyone around to stay home with the
child. Once again, scarcity is, at root, the problem. If there were at least
four adults involved, one of them might well be able to watch baby
while Dad shops. Or if there were plenty of free hours in the day, if
parents didn't need to get to work on time, Dad might happily plunk

himself on the floor to play with baby, even preferring the fun of the game to the chore of shopping. "Later" could become a positive word in his lexicon, not a trigger for conflict. But most parents have neither option available. And so a clash ensues. Parents end up saying, "No, you have to do what I want to do, and you have to do it when I want you to do it!" And toddlers understandably resist and protest.

These moments of struggle over the timing of events are legion: mornings, getting baby ready for childcare while parents try to get to work on time; evenings when parents need freedom to finish a thousand tasks and are desperate to get enough sleep to be able to face the next day. If parents read the battle as willful, if you see the child as arbitrarily saying "No!", then you may well inadvertently teach her that she *is* willful and that willfulness is bad, indeed that she herself is bad.

gendering anger

While struggling awkwardly with the gendered pronoun, I'm also aware of differences between how these dynamics work with boys and girls. Indeed, many of the messages conveyed are about gender. I regularly hear parents complain that, hard as they've tried to protect their young ones from stereotypes of femininity and masculinity, somehow they pick them up and take them on anyway. What you think as a parent about the way your two-year-old conducts business with you cannot but be influenced by your own internalizations of gender. By that I mean that we all take on deep-seated attitudes about who we are and how we're supposed to act, indeed how we're supposed to feel, in our manifestations of girl-ness and boy-ness. Like race in an earlier time, gender today still seems to be a given to most of us, a biological fact beyond shaping or dispute. Yet these assumptions are in fact largely social and historical in nature. Over the past four decades, assumptions about innate characteristics connected with race have been thoroughly challenged (even though they may linger on a more subliminal level in ways that reflect continuing dynamics of racism in our society). Sex-linked matters are more complicated. Recent investigations into hormonal influences that start in the womb and continue through life shed light on a continuum of sex-based characteristics. This research is often cited to prove a reductionist argument that men and women are truly different. But in fact it can better be read, I believe, to add nuance and dimension to our understanding of the interplay between physical and social realities. Biochemical forces interact with interpersonal, cultural, and social ones in elaborate ways. No one element of that dynamic stands alone, in isolation from the others. Training for roles may compound biology or contradict it, depending on where an individual lands on the gender continuum.

In the 1970's and later, sex-based roles were disputed by feminists, among others. There are differences though between gendered roles and gender itself. Very "womanly" women may wear suits and argue powerfully before the Supreme Court, yet they may still embody profound social ideas about how women are supposed to look, move, think, and so on. More recently, "queer culture" has taken on gender directly. With origins in gay liberation movements, the reclamation of the derogatory designation of homosexual as "queer" has come to extend to heterosexual people who refuse to accept characteristics most profoundly associated with straight renditions of gender. "Manly" has come to include effeminate males and muscled female athletes, "womanly" to include muscled female athletes and effeminate males. Transgendered people are pushing the edge of an envelope that is today visible, substantial, on its way to acceptance. In the course of coming out to his parents (who prided themselves on their Sixties radical identity) a high school student I know said pointedly, "You can't consider yourself revolutionary in today's world if you're not challenging gender." He was right. Yet for all the challenges, the daughters of feminists may still love their Barbies and the sons of the gentlest dads may still insist on guns when their birthdays come round.

Let's loop back to a two-year-old fit of anger and trace how some of these gender-shaping messages may be unintentionally conveyed by your reactions. Susan, a single mom, told me with horror about her almost-two-year-old daughter's violent fit. "She flew at me, bit my neck, pulled my hair!," Susan reported with horror. "Afterward," she went on, "I figured out it must really have been grief about her babysitter's disappearance." Martha, the babysitter, had cared for her since her birth and had just left the job.

"But at first I really thought something was wrong with her," the mother reflected.

Compare that with Tracey, whose young son is full of energy and rage. "He bounces off the wall," Tracey said with a wan smile. "I'm exhausted, but I try to just protect myself from getting hurt and let him get it out. He's just a wild, wild boy!"

Lacking an acceptable definition for a "wild, wild girl", Susan was bewildered about how to respond to her distraught daughter. But once the child dissolved into tears, she was able to hold and rock the child. She felt comfortable with the role of nurturing; having found a familiar relationship, she felt relieved and capable. Tracey's male partner, however, sometimes tackles their son, wrestles with him, tickles him, engages physically in all sorts of ways to redirect an angry mood. He too behaves in familiar ways and feels competent.

There have been studies of the ways men and women hold newborn infants differently, cuddling girls as if they were fragile, slinging boys around more athletically earlier in their lives. At the same time, women tend to relate more readily as Susan did, with a nurturing touch while men do rough-and-tumble play. The manner of touch itself conveys gender.

Layer those dynamics with the fact that women still are far more often the primary parent while doing the domestic work of cooking, cleaning, childcare, and so on, and men still far more often relate to children at home through play, and you can see how both the structure of parental relationships and the transactions with children suggest characteristics of gender, whatever the intention of parents. That structural fact of gendered difference is changing, but very, very slowly. More men today share parental duties than in my parenting generation, partly because of a shift in consciousness and partly because of a shift in economic realities. Fewer women nowadays are stay-at-home moms, so the necessity of sharing domestic labor is more urgent. Nonetheless, even when men and women claim in interviews to share domestic duties equally, researchers who actually observe the reality see something quite different. One ground-breaking study of the phenomenon, for example, is Arlie Hochschild's *The Second Shift.*

That such inequalities are persistent is not so surprising, given the tenacity of gender socialization. For one thing, girls are more likely to grow up gaining skills for home and child care, the very things they've experienced doing with their mothers, while boys, tousled by their fathers, are more likely to learn competency in the physical world, as they get older cementing that sense of self by helping men fix things and by participating in team sports. While more girls today do the latter, it is still true that fewer boys do the former. Training for traditional masculinity seems to be harder to alter than training for traditional femininity, perhaps because society needs women who are competent workers, while what goes on in "private" life is primarily of concern to individuals and appears to be irrelevant to the larger society. In this sense and others, the ways of males may appear to be more powerful, and therefore more desirable, than female ways.

"Stuart and I started out determined to share parenting equally," Uma said, "but, boy, have we not ended up that way!"

"Well, you're always a beat ahead of me," Stuart complained, launching into the defense I noted in the last chapter. "I'm glad to do all sorts of things, but you never like the way I do them."

"'A beat ahead of him', ha!," Uma retorted. "Last night the baby was asleep and we were both—finally!—sitting and reading. I heard Cynthia cry and was in the other room and changing her diaper before

Stuart even looked up from his paper. What's *that* about!?"

"I didn't hear her. I really didn't hear her. I was concentrating on the newspaper."

I've cited marketing research studies showing that women, either by training (which I believe is the primary factor) or by brain chemistry, are good at multi-tasking, while men focus on one thing at a time. Domesticity is all about multi-tasking. Perhaps that is why play is a favored activity for men; one rarely wrestles with a toddler and answers the phone and cooks the dinner and folds the laundry all at the same time.

Nor does the gendered nature of the labor market help people equalize the differences in their domestic skill levels. "Besides," Stuart went on, "I'm really tired by the end of the day. I work longer hours than you do, and I guess when I get home I don't want to hear Cynthia cry."

"Don't blame me for that!" Uma quickly protested. "We both decided you should work full time instead of me, because electricians earn so much more money than secretaries do."

Traditionally female jobs still pay less than traditionally male ones. Overall, women today earn 76 cents to men's dollar. While that differential has lessened over the past three decades, most of the change is attributed by economists to a decline in men's wages rather than an increase in women's, largely because of the loss of well-paid unionized blue collar jobs.

All these factors combine to produce one other aspect of these gender dilemmas reflecting back on two-year-old emotional expression. Conflict is their common outcome. I've suggested that the stress of scarcity tends to turn inward, coming home to roost in the most intimate relationships and taking form around lines of difference. Gender is a frequent and highly charged such fault line (although families with same-sex parents may find other kinds of fault lines). By the time a child is two, parents have settled into patterns of conflict; the home fires have become hot and smoky. Meanwhile, the baby is experiencing emotion on the more complex levels that I've described, and s/he is also experimenting with their expression. Whether the child witnesses angry outbursts between parents, or simply feels the smoldering tensions that parents discipline themselves to hide from children's ears, s/he is experiencing their feeling states. Children are intuitive geniuses, until we train it out of them by denying their perceptions and casting doubt on their reality. They are also invested in knowing what goes on around them, having few other means to anticipate what parents will do. At the same time, they have little or no language to identify what they pick up. What they may do instead is channel it, releasing their own tension and yours simultaneously in good, old-fashioned temper tantrums.

3

in a family way:
at home in the early years

With a curl of her lip, Sally Simmons, the diminutive grandmother of two diminutive grandchildren, made clear her disapproval. *"Everything centers around their cozy little family. There's no way in!"*

Sally was protesting, in a somewhat veiled form, what she saw as the controlling behavior of her daughter-in-law. Bonded to the point of isolation with Joe, the son she'd raised alone, Sally unwittingly presented herself as the mother-in-law of myth and fiction: in a battle with the daughter-in-law for possession of her now-grown boy. In fact, though, as we talked more, I saw a rather different drama playing out on a very common stage: the nuclear family.

"I just want time with my grandson. Julia has all these rules: I can't let him out of my sight for a second. I can't get angry at him. I can't keep him overnight!"

Julia told the other side of the story. "She lets Jimmy do whatever he wants, and he's been hurt three times now while he was with her. He's a climber; he's always wanting to go higher than he can. So of course she let him, and he fell out of the tree in her backyard and broke his arm. That was six months ago. Recently, she got mad at him for something or other, and she left him alone while she went to do errands. He's only five, for goodness sake! I was horrified."

So intense were Julia's feelings that they seemed to magnify the space she occupied in the room. In her material form, though, she, like her husband and mother-in-law, was a small person, short and round. Her features sharpened with distress, but her full, warm figure also suggested the nursing mother she was. Joe was only slightly taller than his wife. Like her he carried appealing weight, his face wrinkled around eyes and mouth in a way that suggested his greater comfort with laughter than with anger.

"Sally just can't handle him," Julia continued, in a lower register. "And he *is* a lot to handle." Stories about Jimmy's antics were legion in the community; he was a rip-roarin', risk taking, super energized youngster. "She's grandma, after all, getting up there in years and I think she just gets exhausted and then takes it out on him, like leaving him alone. It's not that I want control, but she's just not up to what it takes."

Julia shot a look at Joe, who sat uncomfortably examining his shoes. "And besides," she went on, shifting grounds for complaint, "I feel bad for Jenny. What can she be feeling when her grandma only wants to be with her brother?!"

It turned out, as we talked further, that a big problem in the family was that Jimmy brutalized Jenny, two years his junior, at every opportunity. While learning to walk, she'd quickly sit down whenever Jimmy came in the room, figuring that he'd knock her over anyway. Now he would pull her hair, rough-house with her, always resulting in her screaming in pain, tease her verbally, and generally assert his superior size.

"She's not passive, though," Julia quickly inserted. "She screams bloody hell and she's constantly coming to get me to intervene. It's exhausting! Guess I can't blame Sally for not wanting to take them both."

Joe grinned and shook his head indulgently. Julia erupted:

"Why don't you say something!" She turned to me. "See what I'm up against? This is what he always does." To Joe, "I want *you* to take Jimmy on. As a matter of fact, I want you to confront *your mother* now and then. You leave all the dirty work to me, and I'm tired of being the bad guy!"

The Simmons family was not as idyllic as they might seem. A list of volatile dynamics and highly-charged problems spewed in every direction.

First, there's the nature of the nuclear family and it's tendency toward isolation, toward turning inward and imagining itself as a self-contained unit, united against the world. At the same time parents juggle an untenable workload, and even when a grandparent who is nearest thing to an extended family lives nearby and wants to participate, the dynamics of competitiveness and control may stand in the way. And children, too, suffer from the absence of people close in their lives. Vibrating with energy, Jimmy was a child who needed many playmates and a great deal of focused adult attention. With nowhere to take his enormous social energy, he turned it toward tormenting the younger sister who was not only an annoying and inadequate playmate but also distracted his mother's attention away from him. I've written an entire chapter on "sibling rivalry" (see chapter 13) so prevalent is it in families, but let me presage my analysis by saying that I view it as a reasonable but ineffective response to legitimate needs and wants which bump up against that constant characteristic of modern families: scarcity. To compete is thoroughly understandable when there is not enough to go around. Far from being a character defect or a symptom of deep-seated psychological problems, it is a practical use of whatever abilities people believe themselves to have: in Jimmy's case, to use his greater size, strength, and verbal ability to engage his sister and at the same time to get his mother's attention (negatively to be sure) through that process.

Second, I suspect you recognized the gendered quality of the conflict between Julia and Joe (not to mention between the children; I'll

address that part in a later chapter). Julia was emotional and outspo-
ken—as was her mother-in-law—while Joe kept a low profile in the
face of conflict, a strategy he may well have learned as a way to handle
his mother and now used to try to deflate his wife's intensity.

"I'm in the middle," he mourned. "I keep trying to find a way
to satisfy both of them, but anything I do is wrong." He explained
that he'd tried to negotiate agreements about how his mother would
oversee Jimmy, but his heart wasn't in it. As a result, Sally was resentful and Julia indignant that he didn't share her anxiety. "I'm just not so
worried," he explained. "Kids break their arms sometimes. True, my
mother's not very attentive to danger and Jimmy's pretty wild. But I'm
sure things will work out in the end. They did for me, even though I
broke a few bones along the way." I could see Julia's jaw quiver as she
clenched her teeth.

Joe's training set him up to be the fixer. He believed he was supposed to mediate, to solve the problem. But Julia only grew angrier
the more he tried. What she wanted instead was for him to share her
perception of the problem and to partner with her in standing up to
Sally. Julia wanted emotional support, and every time Joe came home
with a new way to placate her she felt more alone, less understood, and
more crazed.

Adding to the difficulty was the fact that Joe worked full-time and
Julia was home with the kids all day, every day. She felt she knew the details of the problems, both between the children and with their grandmother, in a way Joe couldn't. He, on the other hand, wanted peace and
fun at home when, finally, he could be there. She was exhausted by the
constant strain of managing the kids' scrapping and fending off what
she saw as her mother-in-law's incursions. She resented that he had all
the fun (as she saw it) and she did all the work at home. Meanwhile, he
was equally exhausted from working, commuting, and taking on additional training to keep competitive in a hardening job market.

Joe and Julia's division of labor embodied very familiar gender lines, tinted though they were by matters of class and race. They could squeeze by financially with one salary while not every family can. Isolation from community more typically afflicts white families, although as more people of color move into the middle class, they too more often find themselves dealing with unpleasantly rigid boundaries surrounding themselves and their children. To a great extent, these boundaries are drawn by the nature of middle-class work. Couples move away from extended families and communities of origin to follow jobs. Or they seek better housing and safer neighborhoods and then find themselves racially isolated in majority-white suburbs. The external nature of those forces are not mysterious. But for white couples, the structures in which they find themselves may seem more "natural," more a consequence of their values and personalities than of the society they inhabit.

Indeed, both Joe and Julia deeply believed themselves to be solely responsible for the well-being of their children. Julia was driven by expectations of mothering instilled by her own upbringing. A cast on Jimmy's arm was a visible sign to the world that she had failed in her duty to protect him. Moreover, when she was unable to intervene successfully to protect Jenny from Jimmy's persecutions, she castigated herself as a weak and ineffective mother.

Joe, too, carried a profile inside his head of what he was supposed to do as husband and father, and that picture was often spattered with self-doubt and uncomfortable recrimination. He wished he could hire a housekeeper to relieve Julia's workload, but he earned too little money. He'd been passed over for a promotion and lost the possibility of a substantial raise any time soon. If he were a better worker, he thought, he might have gotten the promotion. Or at least if he believed in his ability to get a higher salary elsewhere, he might dare to quit. But he knew he made mistakes at work, and somewhere in the recesses of his consciousness there lurked the fear that he was simply not competitive enough, didn't know how to play the political game at work, and so he'd always come out the loser.

But neither Joe nor Julia ever confessed their self-accusations to each other. Indeed, their judgments for each other were too harsh to leave room for very much disclosure of their self-doubts. And so both continued, driven more and more deeply into their roles and less and less resilient in dealing with tensions and problems, ready at the least provocation to be at each other's throats. In a sense, Grandma called the question. She became the lightening rod drawing all that energy.

the rescue triangle

So common are dynamics like these—the harder they struggle the deeper they get mired—that psychologists have named it in a variety of ways. I use a concept invented by a Transactional Analyst named Stephen Karpman called the Rescue Triangle.

In an earlier chapter I outlined guidelines for cooperation. One of those advised against self-sacrifice. The Rescue Triangle is a way to understand patterns of self-sacrifice and their consequences. The concept suggests three roles: Rescuer, Victim, Persecutor. (I use upper case to indicate that I'm using these common words in an uncommon way, as jargon depicting particular concepts.) The idea is that if you play one of those roles, you'll end up playing all the others as well, and in the process you'll find yourself stuck in a self-replicating pattern, a sort of vicious circle with points.

Rescue is defined in two ways: doing things you don't want to do, or doing more than your share of the work in some particular arena. Joe clearly Rescues financially; he is sole supporter of the family. Julia just as clearly Rescues domestically; she does almost all the housework and a far greater share of childcare. She also complains about doing more than her share of the emotional work, dealing with Grandma, trying to stop the children's fights, raising relational issues to Joe, initiating family counseling, and so on.

Each of them does her or his particular form of over-work based in part on the assumption that the other is a Victim, someone lacking the powers needed to be a true partner. Indeed, Julia and Joe agree that she is unable to earn enough money to make a difference. Julia actually has a higher degree than Joe. He barely finished college, she earned a Masters degree in history. But there are not many jobs for MAs in history and the few she sought before their marriage went to more experienced candidates. In this sense, Julia is a victim (with a lower case "v" because I mean it not in a psychological sense but in the common sense, in the world) of a particular labor market. She worked at lower-paid office jobs for awhile, but when the kids arrived she thankfully relinquished wage labor for the work of mothering, a job at which she felt more capable despite undercurrents of self-doubt. Out of the job market now for over five years, she is frightened even to contemplate going back out there. Joe encourages her to apply for jobs she might enjoy – working with kids or helping a non-profit organization that addresses some of the many problems in the world about which she feels strongly. But she's frightened to try. Her fears are what trap her in her role as Victim (with a capital "V"): she has lost confidence in all her many qualities and talents that might translate into hirable skills. Instead of working through her self-doubts, she relies on obvious material impediments to her seeking paid employment. After all, they'd have to pay more for childcare than she'd be able to earn, wouldn't they? So what's the point? Realistic problems intertwine with self-doubt to immobilize her.

Joe goes on being the bread-winner, but with an underlay of resentment.

At first, Julia felt quite good about full-time mothering. When Jimmy was a baby, she took to the task joyfully. She loved nurturing the infant, bathed in the enchantment of his daily discoveries of the world and in the intimacy of his need for her. She knew that Joe couldn't do what she did. He simply lacked the emotional depth to care so attentively. It seemed very right that she mothered while he went to work.

Over time, however, Julia began to miss adult company. She hadn't read a book through to the end for years. Then too, parenting got to be a whole lot less fun when Jimmy turned into a wild two-year-old and, hard on the heels of that transformation, Jenny came along. Jimmy's hostility toward the baby and, Julia increasingly felt, toward her made parenting less thrilling. Increasingly now, she finds herself complaining to Joe, almost before she's realized the extent of her own resentment.

Both parents' resentment signals their journey to the second point of the Triangle: Rescuer turns into Victim. Having accepted a role on the basis of his or her superior capacity to accomplish it, each of them is now burning out. In truth, Joe envies Julia her ability to stay home and engage so thoroughly with the kids. He dreams of all the things he could do with the children if he had time – teach Jimmy about building things, play baseball with him, invent imaginative games with Jenny.

Meanwhile, Julia finds herself remembering the social world she found in the past at work. Even when her jobs were underpaid and beneath her educational status, she enjoyed the interaction with co-workers as well as the intellectual challenge of figuring out office politics. She's tired of the limited dialogue among the young moms she knows. Sometimes she thinks all their brains have been fried by the endless minutiae of dealing with children and housework.

Moreover, each partner's Rescue helps to reinforce the other's role as Victim. If necessity forced Julia to go to work, she'd find a job despite her fears, and maybe, once working, find out that she is after all a competent wage earner. But Joe takes enough edge off their necessity that she can avoid paid labor; the longer she does so, the more she fears and dreads job hunting.

On the other side, Joe has little need or opportunity to learn the subtle language of emotional relationship. When the children skin a knee, they go to Julia, whom they trust to heal and nurture them. Joe can play with the kids, but he freezes when they are upset and need consoling. Similarly, he has few skills to name and work through hard spots with Julia; she's so fast on the draw he rarely if ever experiences the long uncomfortable space that might induce him to learn how to name his feelings.

If Julia and Joe could simply acknowledge their troubles and talk with each other about them, they might entertain some alternatives. But both are convinced there are no alternatives, at least none the other one would accept. And so when they do express discontent, it is aimed at the other person. They move from Victim to Persecutor on the Rescue Triangle.

Persecution takes many forms. Indeed, it engages all the potential of human creativity. Persecutory behavior ranges from overt to covert, the most overt being violence and the most covert being leaving. Joe and Julia were not (yet) at either of those extremes, but Persecutory they surely were. Julia was growing increasingly contemptuous of what she judgmentally labeled Joe's cowardice. How she expressed her distress was to blow her top from time to time: "Why don't you stand up to your mother?! How dare you leave me alone to be the bad guy!"

Meanwhile, Joe was growing increasingly frustrated by what he saw (judgmentally) as Julia's inappropriate anger, not to mention her opportunistic refusal to help with the bills. All the more, he dug in his heels when she went on a diatribe about his mother. The more she moved forward, the more he leaned back. "Yes, dear," is what he said, but in a tone that was patronizing and hostile. He thought of Julia as a princess, she thought of him as a wimp. When not in a resentful frame of mind, in the increasingly brief moments when they could recognize each other as the loved ones they'd known once-upon-a-time, they could formulate more compassionate explanations for the behaviors that they lamented. But in the stress of daily life and their growing desperation for change, they charged each other with critical shortcomings.

But after each outburst, Julia felt guilty, and out of her guilt she resolved to try harder, to be a better mother and wife. So, too, Joe told himself he should be able to stay the course of a "normal" working and home life. After all, his coworkers all did it; why couldn't he? Julia worked so hard, he knew. He should appreciate her more. And so he vowed to be more uncomplaining, more self-sacrificing, to work harder, and censor the part of him that felt ill-used.

This is a book about parenting, so I'll tread lightly on the consequence of all this for sex. No doubt you can fill in that part. Resentment, self-recrimination, and emotional control are a bad trio to take to bed. What solace and re-energizing might accrue from some sweet lovemaking gets lost in the mix, pinned helplessly to the board of Rescue by each and every point in the Triangle.

I'll go on instead to describe some consequences for parenting, illustrating Rescue dynamics in a most frequent arena—the dinner table—and suggesting some routes toward escape.

warring over the brussel sprouts

Food—its preparation, the social rules surrounding its consumption, ideas about nutrition, indeed, everything about it—is a trans-cultural source of conflict. An African-American psychologist once did a hilarious (and painful) riff on the frequency of violence in homes at Thanksgiving time. Mama spends days cooking, everyone eats and drinks too much, someone says something disrespectful of Mama, tempers fray, and eventually people come out swinging, tipping the family into battle.

It sounded all too familiar to me.

Here's the general outline: The parent has internalized (i.e., has learned to believe as axiomatic) the idea that food is an expression both of nurturing and of parental responsibility. That the children eat nutritious food, that they eat at the proper times, that they eat in communion with the family group, are all interlocking injunctions that control a significant part of the parent's time and consciousness.

Most cultures place a powerful value on food. In lands that have known hunger, it represents well-being. Therefore, offering food is an essential gesture of hospitality. I have visited the poorest of poor homes in Bangladesh, places built of reeds and mud, inhabited by rail-thin adults and pot-bellied, bow-legged children. I knew without doubt that the larder consisted of little more than a handful of rice, if that.

Nonetheless, over all the guest's protests, a boy would be sent to the tea stand to buy one biscuit, another dispatched up a palm tree to harvest a coconut for its cool, sweet milk. Not to offer food would be the worst of defeats, admission of total abjectness.

In America, parents often add to the social exchange represented by feeding children a thick set of ideas about good nutrition. Children should get so much protein, so many vegetables, and such and such fiber. They should not eat sweets before meals lest their appetite be hijacked. If they indulge their natural taste for sugar, their teeth will rot. Assaulted by self-contempt for what they view as their own lack of control over weight, they fear the "obesity epidemic," a phantom of national proportions much debated in the media as I write.

And so parents spend great chunks of time shopping, cooking, serving, and washing up—Rescuing in the sense of doing more work than they want to do, and also, according to the other definition, doing more than their share of the work of knowing and meeting children's physical needs. All that effort is based on the assumption that children, left to their own devices, will eat all of the wrong things. This mistrust of nature, the idea that youngsters lack a self-regulating mechanism capable of recognizing their bodies' needs and responding appropriately, dictates a determination to assume control of this most basic of bodily processes. Meanwhile, kids resist. Not only do they feel deprived of tasty things, but they also resent the detailed control of their behaviors by their parents. So parent (usually still mother, but increasingly also father) slaves over a hot stove preparing a superbly balanced meal....and kids refuse to eat it.

"I don't like brussel sprouts!," they cry. "I only want mashed potatoes. That meatloaf is yucky! Can't I just have dessert?"

"Eat your vegetables!," parents insist. "No dessert until you finish what's on your plate."

So distracting is the power struggle that appetite, tastes, and bodily needs are overridden by the social dynamics that seize the dinner table.

Now layer those dynamics with the added injunction that dinner is supposed to be a social time, the one chance in a crowded day for the family to gather and actually relate.

"How was school today, Jimmy?"

"OK, I guess."

"Did you learn anything interesting?"

"No."

"Did you play any fun games?"

"I guess."

Jimmy's minimalist responses represent a child's form of Persecution. He might not be able to gain supremacy over his appetites, but he's damn well not going to cede conversational ground.

"I want to watch TV. Can't I go now?"

Sometimes the drama is further layered by cultural agendas. Immigrant parents may want to preserve connections with the land of their origins by serving foods familiar in the homeland. But Americanized kids want pizza or hot dogs. Rice? Yuck! Delicately spiced lentils? Feed them to Grandma; I don't want them!

Then, once again, there's gender: women tend to absorb more sense of responsibility about feeding people, seeing it as a form of nurturing as well as an area of expertise. Men may be more adamant about conversation at dinner, deprived of contact as they may be both because they do not participate as much in the connections afforded by caretaking, and, even if they do the tasks, may not view them as constituting a relationship. So dinner conversation fills a crucial place for them, and their anger at their offspring's refusal to talk is all the greater. But the more Mom invests in her cooking, the more Dad relies on his talking, the more kids feel overpowered and under-appreciated. *How come the parents don't trust me to eat right and don't want me to do what I want to do, like eat in front of the TV set? Grown-ups want it all their own way!*

Kids experience themselves as Victims to their parents' agendas. And meanwhile, parents come to feel Victimized when kids reject their offerings and negate the benefits of parental hard work. Parents react angrily by chastising kids, who in turn just want all the more to escape. And so on the next night, beset by guilt for her unpleasantness the night before, Mom tries to prepare a more enticing menu, while Dad, contrite in his own way, casts about for more engaging conversational topics. Met with complaints and silence, they get angrier still and round and round it goes.

One helpful way to view these dynamics is in terms of power. The person in charge of the kitchen assumes the power—right along with the responsibility—of making choices by exercising her own opinion about what to eat and when, how to cook it, and how much of it is enough or too much. Being in charge of food may even be the one way that women do feel powerful. Trapped at home, unable to find adequate respect and acknowledgment in an external world that demeans domestic labor, women take to heart the housewifely duties they are assigned, wanting to do them to the hilt of perfection. So profoundly socialized is the inclination to judge oneself by standards of perfectionism at home that I've found even women highly successful in their wage-earning lives driven by them. And, in turn, they drive their mates and kids to exhaustion, as well as themselves. Indeed, I've couched this story in terms of a gender division of labor more purely characteristic of an earlier generation (although increasing re-occurring in young families today) in part to highlight themes of stress that so often survive into restructured, two-earner families.

Meanwhile, the person defining eating time as family-togetherness time assumes the power to set the venue for meals as well as the conversational requirements. Here too, the desire to capture table time for re-establishing connection may be all the stronger if a parent regrets having to be away from home so much of the day.

On the other hand, resistance is also powerful. All those acts of refusal—not eating the veggies, not answering the questions—serve to undermine parental power and seize a measure of it back.

Each family member thus enjoys a certain set of abilities, of powers, and also experiences oppression. Each joins in a conclusion that his or her alternatives are limited and therefore continues to do the particular behavior that traps her or him in the Rescue drama.

So what's the way out? How to escape the inevitability of the Rescue Triangle?

There are two answers: First is to seek ways to expand your options. How can the work of food preparation be minimized? How could working parents manage to spend more time with their kids? Clearly, these changes would challenge some very fundamental structures of life. They speak for more adult involvement, perhaps more money, very likely more time. Each of these factors may seem idealistic, but if we can't imagine the ideal, then we can be certain we won't achieve it.

In my case, after I returned to the U.S., my sense of the possible was informed by my experience of extended family and community in India. A close friend of mine, Becky, had become involved in an alternative form of psychotherapy. Based on ideas about alienation rather than mental illness, the approach placed a high premium on community. Between Becky's theoretical orientation and my practical experience at the beginning of parenting—despite both our trepidations—we set about to invite our closest friends to join us in a grand experiment: living collectively.

For the next eighteen years, through marriages and divorces, career changes and joys and crises, we constituted a joint household. Life was not perfect, but it was hugely improved compared with single parenthood, or even two-parent parenting. One enormous gift to me was the introduction of Joshua into my life. I regularly claim two sons, for Josh had just turned one when we first met. He's in his thirties now, and still one of my two kids.

What greater numbers of adults give you is a lot more room to exercise the second "way out" of Rescue: negotiate. Theory has it that among eight people someone will always have the energy and the desire to do whatever needs to be done; no one needs to Rescue. But even with greater limitations of labor, creative arrangements can often be found. If each position on the Triangle embodies a power stance, then power-sharing is a practical alternative. I'll play out a hypothetical dialogue around the dinner table, not as any sort of definitive answer, but just to suggest some strategies.

Solutions start with expression. Straight talk about what each person feels and wants almost always surfaces unrecognized possibilities. There is a slogan connected to the notion of the Rescue Triangle, to help people find their way out: Ask for 100% of what you want, 100% of the time ... and then negotiate. What we more often do is to compromise in the first act of negotiating. "I couldn't possible ask him/her to do that, so I'll only ask for this lesser thing." Once you've given up some more in the course of working through a solution, you are in jeopardy of finding you've compromised too much, creating a strong likelihood that, sooner or later, you'll rebel and unilaterally renege.

To learn to ask for what you really want, parents may have to overcome some assumptions, especially the one about the inevitability of health disaster if kids are trusted more to choose what they eat. For the moment, try to suspend disbelief. If you have a clearer idea of the rewards, the work of rethinking such imbedded assumptions becomes more palatable.

Julia: "I used to enjoy cooking. Now all the joy has gone out of it. What I'd really like is to cook a meal only once in a while, when I'm inspired. And I'd like to really know what you all want to eat so I can cook things you appreciate."

Joe: "I don't much care what we eat. But I really miss being in on your day. Most of all, I'd like to engage with you kids. Actually, I'd be happier if we were down on the floor playing a board game or building a model."

Jimmy: "I want to eat things I like, and I don't want to sit at the table all the time when I eat. I don't always want to talk to you, but I do want to play with you and go places with you and watch TV with you. I also really like hearing you read me a story at bedtime, and cuddling with you while I fall asleep."

The next step is to talk about concerns:

Julia: "Well, I worry that you'll get sick if you only eat things you like. You don't seem to like some of the things that I believe are good for you, like veggies and meat. And when you eat a lot of sweets or drink sugary sodas, you get very hyper, a sign your body's out of balance. Not to mention that you're a drag to be around when you're so manic. I need peace and quiet at night, not a kid bouncing off the walls. In fact, after all the shopping and cooking I do, I'm usually too tired to play with you, so I'll miss getting together at the dinner table."

Joe: "You know, I'm with you, Jimmy, about doing all those things together. But your mother knows more about nutrition, so if she's worried about that, I guess I should be, too."

Jimmy: "I don't want you to be mad at me all the time if I don't eat what you cook."

Next, start looking for solutions that might take care of all of you. Maybe Julia should do less shopping and cooking. Maybe, if she really wants to cook for herself, she should do that without expectation that others will eat with her. There was a time when we invited our kids to let us know by late afternoon whether they planned to eat with us, or at least to eat what the grown-ups cooked. If we didn't hear from them, we assumed the answer was no. Meanwhile, we stocked healthy cereals, un-sugared peanut butter, whole wheat bread, and other reasonably healthy, easily prepared foods, and we stored them at child level in the kitchen. The kids were on their own. They learned very early how to boil an egg, make toast, even mix up a yummy tuna salad. And when they got tired of doing that, they let us know they wanted to share what we cooked.

Amazingly, we began to notice that the kids were eating less ice cream, drinking less soda. They grew to recognize the signs that they were hungry and to pay attention to cravings that signaled nutritional needs. They would often go for several days eating only one food group, stuck on toast or string beans or cold chicken. Just when we'd start to get nervous, they'd move on to the next food type. Overall, they balanced out their body's needs. As adults, they eat very well, preferring healthy foods to junk. I suspect they were influenced by seeing the adults around them eat (reasonably) healthy foods, as well as having access to good food themselves. I often think they naturally gravitate to a better diet than I do. Given my more rigid dietary upbringing, with its insistence on proportions of foods that have since been revised, I usually have to think about what I should eat rather than listening and responding to my body.

That is the crucial point: few children, left to their own devices, will either go hungry or deprive themselves of necessary nutrients for very long. Newborns know when they need to feed and how much to nurse. When do they unlearn that wisdom? How do we, the adults around them, teach them to mistrust their body language, to opt for the wrong foods? I believe we do that by applying our own eating rules —indeed, not "our own" in the sense that they come from our body knowledge, but rather in that we've been taught to believe they are right. We over-write a baby's relationship with her or his own body by saying, "Not now," and "That's enough." Allowed to discover the language of the stomach, children naturally balance out their food needs. The responsibility of adults is to provide healthy alternatives, not to dictate choices, timing, or amounts of food. The benefits of parents' faith that youngsters can feed themselves wisely far outweigh the liabilities of an occasional stomach ache or a sped-up evening. Allowing small kids their own exploration of eating is not only useful in its own right, but it is a model for parenting. It means you are not seeing the child as a Victim, someone lacking the ability to learn, and you are not Rescuing by taking too much control of the wrong things. Instead you are exercising responsibility by shopping wisely, and then staying out of the way. Best of all, you are not mired in escalating spirals of resentment and recrimination.

Food is a complex matter; it means more than fueling the body. Have you ever been advised to stop nursing an infant because, "She's not really hungry; she just wants comforting"? How did you know that was true? If it was true, what does it benefit to sever the link between food and nurturing? All those cultures that use food for hospitality, celebration, and conviviality are simply continuing something every infant knows: food connects people at the same time that it gives sensual pleasure.

In the weight-phobic West, we fear acknowledging the usefulness of food for nurturing because, I believe, our need for nurturing seems a bottomless pit. If we get so little, if we live lives that are so blanched of pleasure, then we may not be able to judge the balance point between body satisfaction and the satisfaction of the spirit. And so we malign and eliminate eating, starving ourselves on both planes of existence; and then when we cannot hold back any more—we gorge.

I've said that children, left to their own devices will eat reasonably well. Of course, few children are left to their own devices. I've already emphasized the practicalities of access to food. Culinary traditions can skew taste. Then, too, there is advertising, a constant barrage of inducement to eat the most sugary cereal and the least healthy burgers and sodas. My example of the two-year-old toddler raising a storm in pursuit of Popsicles is an example of the power of merchandising. It's no accident that sweet things are displayed in glass cases and in racks right at the check-out stand.

The concept of Rescue is most helpful when looking closely at small numbers of people in relationship with each other. It becomes less useful in situations where people really are victims, not Victims in the definition of the Triangle. Bombardment by skillful advertising claims has the power to turn Victims (children seen to be unable to choose for themselves) into victims (people whose good sense is overwhelmed by the inducements of propaganda). There are many ways in which people in most societies are in fact victims to some form of oppression or injustice. There is still, today—despite dedicated efforts by many people to overcome racism—discrimination in many forms against people of color. Women do still often earn less money than men for comparable skill levels and quality of labor. Children are vulnerable to crime in the streets, to road danger, to family isolation. Imagine the difference if kids had several choices of families with whom to live. We'd have a lot more peaceable world, simply because both parents and kids had options.

Factoring into the equation of Rescue consumerist pressure on children to eat unhealthy things, where is the line between control and guidance? One place to seek it is in the realm of explicit criticism. One of my major goals in rearing children was to help them cultivate the power of critique. I knew I couldn't endlessly protect them from all the many things I objected to in the culture, from candy to racism, from demeaning language to sexism. What I could do was demonstrate the power of an opinion, of *my* opinion and by extension of *their* opinion. "Why do you suppose," I'd ask rhetorically, "they're showing that cute bear eating that super-sweet cereal? I think it's because they want to trick kids into buying their brand." Then I'd offer some healthful cereal smothered in fresh fruit that I knew they really liked. "Just as good, huh? I actually like it a whole lot better," I'd prompt.

Okay, so I was pitting my propaganda against "their" propaganda. My defense is that my kids knew they had the ability to disagree with me, but the form of the discussion between us, the very fact they could answer back, prompted them to make a thoughtful argument. And that's what I was after. I didn't think they'd die an early and hideous death if they ate a bowl of sugar-coated flakes. I was willing to take that risk. I thought the higher value was in urging them to consider alternatives and justify their choice.

There was a way in which I did not share power with them altogether. Parents hold the very considerable power of the purse strings.

I did ultimately have the ability to refuse to pay for foods I didn't like. When they got a little older and had access to money, they could buy whatever they wanted themselves, if they wanted it enough to spend their own money on it. They rarely did. Money is a realm for contesting power in which adults have a real advantage. In my family there was room for negotiation, but the bottom line was the grown–ups' refusal to buy those things about which we felt most strongly—toy guns and violent games. In fact, violence was for us the line we wouldn't cross. Food was a bit more malleable, but it remained true that we adults held the ultimate power. We weren't willing to change that radically, but we were willing to admit it. "I know you really want that cereal, but, you know what, I just think it's so icky that I can't bring myself to buy it. I know that's not so fair, but that's how it is. Here's what you can do, though. You can choose between Brand A and Brand B, and I'll buy what you want most."

broadening the family

I've focused on the family dinner table because it typifies dynamics within nuclear families. My own choice to live in a more collective household was inspired by my experience of extended family in India, joined with counter-culture experiments in collectivity we were witnessing all around us. For many Americans, though, alternative examples are hard to find. Older models of extended families (which still exist for many people closer to more collectivist old countries from which they more recently immigrated), young couples living with in-laws or joining with siblings and their partners to buy otherwise-unaffordable housing, are beginning to re-emerge, driven by economic necessity as much as by social vision. Rewarding as it might be, living collectively is neither possible nor desirable for everyone.

In the course of my work as a therapist and mediator, though, I've encountered numbers of imaginative and effective experiments with family structure.

neighborly collaboration

Perhaps the simplest model depends on luck: finding yourself living next door to a family with children close in age to your own. Hasan and Matilda bought a home in an inter-racial, middle-class neighborhood on the southern border of a large city. Semi-suburban but close to urban transportation, the community maintained a tradition of friendly welcome to newcomers. While the moving trucks were stilled parked outside, Sylvia walked over with a plate of cookies. "Could you use some dinner tonight? I'm making spaghetti and could easily double the recipe?" Matilda gratefully accepted, and the links were begun. Before summer was over, Sylvia and another woman up the block organized a block party, so that the new family could meet their neighbors.

Soon, Sam and Max, and Nancy and Fred had become a pack. The kids were back and forth to each others homes. None of the parents was entirely comfortable with children on the sidewalk in front of their row houses. Neighborly though their surroundings might be, it was nonetheless a busy street, lots of traffic and unknown passersby. Matilda and Sylvia took themselves to the hardware store one day and figured out how to install a gate in the fence separating their backyards. The children requested another so they could join classmates whose house, though around the block, backed on Sylvia's yard. There were now seven children, in various combinations of size, age, race, gender, who played together safely in backyards.

It didn't take long for all the parents to realize the potential for exchanging childcare. A single mom, Sylvia initiated the practice. "I hesitated to ask at first," she said later, "because I saw it as needy, as asking for help no one else needed since they were all coupled.

"It came as a surprise—at least until we all talked about it at some point—that they were so receptive. We realized that they were as desperate for help as I was, they just didn't think they should be, so they didn't ask."

Breaking the ice to negotiate cooperative arrangements like these often falls to single parents. Rather than reflecting dysfunctional neediness, I see it as a major contribution to two-parent families, a form of leadership born of necessity that is more recognizable for unpartnered parents but almost as severe for others.

sharing childcare

Right away when Stephanie called me with questions about a mediation, I knew I'd be dealing with people after my own heart. They were four families, she explained, each with two parents and two children. Sound average? They were anything but. Some years ago, Michael and Stephanie were working in the same office when Stephanie became pregnant and Michael told her his wife, Natalie, was just about as far along as she.

"We all got together and we hit it off real well," Stephanie said. "It was great to have other parents-to-be to talk with, especially about how to deal with combining work and childcare." Her partner, Naomi, was especially conflicted. She really wanted to have significant time with the baby, but she was also on the fast track toward partnership in the law firm she'd joined just two years back.

Natalie and Michael had made a deal that she'd get to stay home for the first six months, but they both knew she'd have to go back to work then if they were to survive financially. Stephanie and Michael had already started conversations at work with their peers about lobbying for flex time and paternity leave.

"We hit on this idea of sharing childcare. My brother and sister-in-law were also expecting. And Natalie and Michael's next door neighbors were a lesbian couple with a new baby. So we invited them to join us for some strategizing."

What they worked out was a plan to hire a nanny jointly, and for one of the eight parents to work with her each day. That way, no one needed to be off work more than a day about every two weeks. Naomi opted for less frequency than that; in return, she handled "personnel" matters, collecting dues, paying the nanny, spearheading hiring and reviews and what-have-you.

"It sounds great!" I said on that initial phone conversation. "Where's the conflict?"

"Well, it's about holidays. Our lives have gotten steadily more enmeshed, and now we're having trouble sorting out who goes where on the holidays."

Since that beginning, each couple had produced a second child, inspiring each other to similar timing. Before long, the older kids had begun to insist on time with the other children outside childcare hours, and especially over the holidays. The parents had been pleased at first. They'd consulted about joint plans for part of Christmas day, for massive Easter egg hunts involving nieces and nephews and friends' children as well as their own, and so on. They'd agreed to celebrate Hanukah, Chinese New Year, and Kwanzaa as well.

By that time, their own relatives were complaining. When would they go to Grandma and Grandpa's house? Planning got increasingly complex. Finally, Michael and Stephanie's sister-in-law crossed swords, each insisting on her or his particular needs. Couple loyalties and rifts began to develop. Themes of culture showed up, including some of the lesbians' fears that some of the heterosexual people assumed their needs to be more important, that they were "real families" as opposed to....

At this point, Naomi and Stephanie proposed mediation, a method they'd used to resolve some conflicts between them over the years. I met with all eight parents for two long sessions, and we laid out all the grievances, connected all the interlocking dots of emotion and interpretation, surfaced biases and assumptions so they could be worked through, traced out and derived lessons from all the communication-gone-awry, and worked out a set of agreements about how to conduct these innovative and increasingly profound relationships, as well as schedules for the coming holidays.

Last I heard, the child-care community was going strong. Naomi and Stephanie were planning their third pregnancy, and Naomi was determined this time to take a year away from her firm, where she was now a full partner.

co-housing

In the early 1970s, when I first returned to the U.S from India, I lived in a working-class apartment project in Northern California. We had a pleasant townhouse apartment facing a lovely hillside where children could play, safe from traffic and strangers. There was a tiny swimming pool; tenants gathered there whenever possible and the parents in the complex watched out for each others' kids. Tuhin always had playmates around, and I soon formed friendships with two other single moms.

Meanwhile, I was talking with old friends and colleagues about living arrangements. They were two couples with babies, all the adults working and going nuts trying to balance responsibilities, as well as a single woman who wanted no children but was dedicated to having them in her life.

My apartment project became a model for us of a way to live. Imagine a complex populated by like-minded people, all of us committed to building community together! We could each have our own home, as well as sharing spaces for our more collective activities.

In the end, we couldn't find such housing that was affordable, and we relented and moved in together under one roof. Collective living proved both challenging and enormously worth it, but the vision of this other, more village-like structure continued its appeal.

Years later, we began to hear of a model initiated in Scandinavia called co-housing. Groups of people were actually buying land in cities all over America and working with commercial developers to build small homes and larger shared spaces. Some had communal kitchens, as well as recreation spaces, rooms for house guests, shared laundry facilities, big kitchen gardens, or whatever residents wanted. One such community was built in a warehouse across the Bay from San Francisco. Another group acquired a number of homes on a single block. Others popped up in other out-lying communities where land was affordable. Some negotiated for funding to subsidize mixed-income housing.

One project I visited was started by friends of mine in Atlanta. Eleanor Smith is a wheelchair user. Over many years I'd heard from her her experiences of the hardship of exclusion from most homes. For example, Eleanor had raised my awareness about the oppression produced by the width of standard bathroom doors—too narrow for a wheelchair, too far from facilities to manage without access. Visiting friends becomes an exercise in discomfiting control, or embarrassing need.

Eleanor founded an organization called Concrete Change, their mission being the creation of policy to require that all new homes be accessible. Her group has led the state of Georgia in pioneering such engineering.

Meanwhile, Eleanor and her partner joined with other people to build a marvelous co-housing community. Every living space, every communal structure, is accessible. For the first time in her life, Eleanor can drop in casually on friends and neighbors. Now housing families with children, single people, young and old, the project stands as proof of the possibility for humane communities.

The chance to design physical space to meet human needs is rare and thrilling. Safe communities for kids—no cars, trusted neighbors, shared child-friendly spaces—allow parents relief from some of the most common, structurally imposed problems of parenting. Most of all, these communities overcome scarcity. If there are enough willing hands and hearts, enough of the support that young families need and deserve, no one need Rescue so dramatically that burnout and Persecution can result.

the moral of the story

Think innovation. Pin to your bathroom mirror the slogan, "Necessity is the mother of invention." Physical structure bespeaks social structure, and the ones we are given strongly tend to isolate us in untenable family arrangements. Breaking out and connecting up with others may be hard, but it does a world of good.

As I write, the Simmons challenged the structure of their nuclear family, big time: they moved to a small town. Jimmy can walk to school by himself; he's become an articulate, humorous, and eminently negotiable youngster. Julia has a job working with children in a neighborhood health clinic. When they first moved, Joe had trouble finding work. He became a stay-at-home dad for a while, learning to do many of the things both he and Julia had always assumed he was incapable of doing. They struggled a bit about his doing them his way, not Julia's, but over time Julia became convinced the kids were fine and Joe's approaches were viable. Now, Joe comes home from his job daily to give the kids lunch. He's thinking of taking a cooking class.

Jenny's now the rambunctious four-year-old, but unlike her brother at that age, she runs off energy playing with a small pack of small children all day long. All four of the Simmons have learned to know their needs, to talk, to negotiate. They live a lot further away from Grandma Sally, and when they do see her, they're a lot more welcoming of her relationship with the kids.

4

managing separation anxiety:
early school years

> Developmental challenges:
>   1) Balancing work and home
>   2) Negotiating social identities

So far, I've focused on parenting within the four walls of home and the ways that parents might manage to go beyond that structure. Now I want to address those interfaces with the outside world that are not entirely voluntary. For many families in the years between two and five, and for almost all families in the years after five, raising children is an operation in negotiating institutions beyond the home. School for kids, workplaces for grown-ups, both confront parents with a whole set of other needs for negotiation skills and emotional literacy.

Let's start with the earliest interface between family and the outside world. You go back to work after your parental leave is over; what form of childcare do you put in place? And how do you feel about it?

stretching the cord

However short or long the time you've had to be with your baby, the transition back into the world of work is complicated. I hear new parents reacting sometimes with relief, but more often with anxiety. On the most basic level, there is an intensity to being focused on a small child. It compels the attention, both because the bonding (not to mention the fascination) is unlike any other and also because the labor required to care for an infant or toddler is so constant. For a month or six months or two years or more, you've carried the child in the forefront of your consciousness. Whatever else you might have done during that time was fitted in around the needs of the baby.

There is a pace to infant care that is very different from the pace of most jobs. Doing laundry and cooking alternate with nursing or bottle-feeding, activity alternates with stillness. Joyful play gives way to unexpected emotional storms; from delighting in baby's laughs you're suddenly plunged into the mystery of an indecipherable need. Nature may not be your only metronome during this period, but it is surely the dominant one.

Then, from one day to the next, there you are back in wage-earner-time mode, working to the rhythms of the job rather than peristalsis. New parents often find themselves seriously distracted in the first days back on the job. Who am I? What am I supposed to be doing here? What's happening back home or at childcare? Is the baby crying for me? Feeding well? Happy or frightened? It's hard to re-find habits of concentration that came easily before.

Then too, many parents feel resentment that they're back in harness so soon. Some European countries afford new parents far longer leave than is common in the U.S.. Sweden, for instance, gives parents fifteen months of leave during which time their job is protected and they are paid 80 percent of their salary. Nor must they take leave only at the time of birth; the offer stands until the child is eight. Norway offers nearly a year at full pay.

In the U.S., on the other hand, federal law mandates twelve weeks without pay, during which time a job is guaranteed. Taking longer requires strategy and sacrifice. Humane social policies result from a combination of shared societal values and successful social movements. Why, we might ask, has more not been secured in America? One theory I would posit is that the strains of individualism and a religious morality of self-sustenance intertwine to undercut ample support for parents of young children.

Simone is a single mom. When she was expecting, she applied for a year's sabbatical at partial pay from her public school teaching job, a highly competitive process negotiated into the contract by the teachers' union. By good luck (and, I suspect, by virtue of the very good reputation she'd amassed over twelve years of teaching), she was selected. By combining maternity leave with the sabbatical, and adding on the summer vacation, she was able to construct a Sweden-like introduction to motherhood.

As the time to go back to work approached, Simone agonized over arrangements. She visited dozens of childcare centers. But the ones she liked best only took kids who were out of diapers. One or two that seemed feasible would require enormously long commutes from home to childcare to work. Beyond the time and stress involved, Simone couldn't abide the thought of being so far away from her little girl, Siena. "What if something happened," she queried anxiously, "it would take me forty-five minutes just to get to her!"

In the end, Simone managed to hire a grandmotherly woman to care for the baby at home. "I just decided it was worth it to me to divide my salary in half and hire Francesca. We liked each other right away, and Siena seemed entirely comfortable with her."

Simone had stashed away some money for a someday-down-payment on a home, but she decided it was better spent giving Siena the excellent care—and herself the peace of mind—that first year back at work.

My friends and I had to overcome considerable fear along the way as we traveled the path from separate households to collective living. What finally pushed us over the edge was a scene that vividly expressed how Joshua felt about impersonal childcare arrangements. For the most part, one or another of the adults that had formed community stayed with the children when parents were away. The rare times when none of us were available, we hired a teenage baby-sitter. She was a sweetheart, red haired, freckle-faced, competent, and fun. Both Tuhin and Josh loved playing with her. But one night when all three of their collective parents (Josh's dad Don was a central person in our group) went out together, we returned home to find Tuhin asleep on the sofa and the babysitter quietly weeping in a corner. Josh, just short of two at the time and a child of great heart and attachment, had refused to go to bed before we came home. He'd gotten more and more upset and, unable to comfort him, the babysitter had become more and more frantic. Desperate, she'd seated him on his beloved tricycle, a recent gift. There he was, little fingers gripping the handlebar, face smeared with tears and snot, his frame still heaving with occasional sobs, fast asleep.

We believed the problem was that Josh was unwilling to accept a caretaker who didn't appear in his life at any other times, for any other purposes. We sensed the legitimacy of that reaction.

We drove the teenager home and vowed to move in together, to provide a large enough pool of parents that someone would always be available for caretaking.

Other people accomplish similar goals by other means. Stephanie and her gang formed a childcare collective. Cindy and Carolina got Cindy's mom to agree to baby-sit for the first two years before they even began insemination. Charles put his as-yet unborn child's name on the waiting list for the on-site childcare center where he worked, one of the few offered by a company in the city where he lived. Santhia found herself divorced with two small children and very little financial help from their father. She started a small childcare business in her home, caring for as many as five children, including her own, and providing herself with the opportunity to be a stay-at-home mom and to earn enough to pay the rent all in one sweep.

Older sisters, elderly aunts, hired workers willing to take on two or three babies at a time: working parents try a range of possible solutions.

Hopefully, your own arrangements work out well enough to reassure you. But that's not the end of the problem. There's the issue of socializing a baby to industrial time, getting a young one up and fed and clothed and transported all in the wee hours before you're due at work. There's the need for family leave when the child is sick, the problem of coordinating childcare holidays with alternative arrangements, the difficulty of leaving work on time when that special rush project comes along and the baby must be picked up by six o'clock.

Life for working parents is a constant juggling act, requiring skills of management and negotiation far surpassing those of career diplomats.

So while you're dealing with separation anxiety, you're also, in other ways, in continuous mental touch with your child. Even if you're one of those parents who is relieved to be back in the world of adults, especially with a paycheck attached, you're likely to experience a fair amount of tension between your roles. The umbilical cord turns out to be made of rubber; it stretches, but it's always right on the verge of snapping back at you.

school and identity

As your child grows older, school becomes increasingly a site for complex interaction. Erik Erikson, like many other developmental psychologists after him, places the development of social identity in the teen years. My experience tells me something else; it starts here, at the very beginning of life-in-the-world.

Siena's mother Simone is African-American; Siena's father Guillermo is of Mexican heritage. Even though he and Simone ended their relationship before the baby was born, Guillermo is devoted to Siena and sees her regularly, as does his mother. United in wanting to promote bilingualism, all three adults make a point of speaking Spanish to the child.

Simone and Siena share an apartment with another single mom and her two kids just on the border of an affluent, largely white neighborhood. The local elementary school is coveted by many parents. Simone feels very lucky to live inside its district.

But soon after Siena starts kindergarten, she begins to seem depressed. Simone asks her often how things are at school, and Siena answers, "OK. Do I have to go tomorrow?" Simone talks to the teacher, a pleasant white woman, well experienced at her job, who reports that Siena seems to be having some trouble connecting to the other children for no apparent reason.

One evening, Siena looks up from a coloring book and asks, "Mama, what's wrong with Spanish?"

"Nothing's wrong with it," Simone responds emphatically. "Who told you there is?"

"Well, when I speak it at school, nobody answers me."

Siena's bilingual world has suddenly bumped up against a monolingual classroom.

Now Simone begins to notice other troubling signs. Siena is coloring a little girl in her coloring book, using blue for the eyes and yellow for the long, straight hair. Siena's eyes are shining black, and her hair is a tight cap of dark curls. Simone looks through some other coloring books and finds the color schemes all similar.

"How about coloring the next girl to look like you," she suggests. Siena remains silently scribbling the page.

"Want me to help you?" Simone asks.

Siena shakes her head without looking up.

"Why not?" Simone persists.

"Not supposed to," Siena mumbles. She closes the book and scatters the crayons around the room. Added to her concerns about racial ideas Siena may be developing, Simone now wonders where her wonderfully free and adventuresome daughter learned the concept of "supposed to."

Five-year-olds moving from sheltered worlds of cultural consistency may encounter issues of race and language without preparation in kindergarten. Children are brilliant observers of their social worlds. They interpret data with complex sensitivity, drawing conclusions that are sometimes painful. Because she is in a racial and cultural minority in her school, Siena has noticed that blue-eyed, straight-haired little girls are either more prevalent, or, more likely, subtly better appreciated, than children who look like her. Perhaps her white teacher compounds the message, just by virtue of her identity as leader. Aides in the class may be dark-skinned, such that Siena has translated a professional hierarchy into a social one.

Categorization comes naturally to very young children. It is part of developing language, as well as skills of observation and conceptualization. At twenty-two months, Lucy's favorite word was "similar." The little girl coming to visit was "similar to Lucy." A first taste of brie offered by Grandma was "similar to cheese." My all-time favorite was an armored truck pictured in Lucy's book that, she noted, was "similar to an armadillo."

Fun as Lucy's categorization was (I hope for her, though certainly for the grown ups), not all observations like these are pleasurable. We live in a world of hierarchies. Stratification is enforced on a psychological level by all sorts of judgments and values that attach to different locations in the social order. Children notice and apply to themselves and the adults around them fine-grained understandings of these rankings of worth and power. At the very beginning, children begin to sort themselves and their world into categories of greater and lesser desirability.

Some years ago, I conducted a study of race relations in a southern state in the 1950's. Interviewing people who'd grown up at the time, I discovered a profound difference in white and black children's earliest experiences of race. Because life was so thoroughly segregated, most black children grew up in protected communities where they rarely if ever saw white people. First encounters, especially for boys, often happened at an age when they first ventured downtown. Time after time, men told me stories of being called names by older white boys when they were young. Fifty years later, their voices still tightened with pain.

More subtly, people described noticing how a parent was treated by white people by being made to sit in the back of the bus or addressed as "boy" by a bus ticket seller.

White people who grew up at the same time told a very different story. For them, their first experience of racial difference was with a black maid in their home. She nurtured and served them; their parents were clearly her boss. The very structure of acquaintanceship—nurturing at home by a servant or hostility in public places from older children—taught searing lessons about the racial order in society.

Today, the sharp edges of racial ordering have been moderated. But now we deal with new versions, with what Valerie Batts, the founder of Visions, Inc., a diversity training organization, calls "modern racism." It operates less overtly but just as surely, through silences and complex Rescues and disaffection of the sort five-year-old Siena was encountering in kindergarten. The asymmetry of experience people in my study experienced still exists, albeit in very different forms. Already by kindergarten age, many children of color know they are being identified as "different" while white children know they are the standard by which difference is measured.

This phenomenon of learning how we're supposed to be, and what it means about us if we fail to live up to the standard, is sometimes called internalized oppression. Siena's example of learning a derogatory view of herself is the most obvious form that it takes. But all children internalize stories about the world and about themselves in it, and very often aspects of that process involve a diminished sense of possibility. We all have multiple identities—a variety of ways to define ourselves. Different aspects of identity get activated in different circumstances. Similarly, we take instruction about how we're supposed to act, given who we are, in many different ways.

Take the story in the previous chapter. What do Jimmy and Jenny learn from Julia's multiple Rescues of them? Julia is the most conscientious of mothers, wholly committed to nurturing her children's self-esteem and creativity. Yet the circumstances of their lives combined with Julia's own learned ideas about mothering to create dilemmas and contradictions.

The more she acted out her principles about good nutrition, the more she might be communicating to them distrust for their own relationship to their needs. The more she protects Jenny from Jimmy's roughness, the more she may be teaching Jimmy that he's bad and Jenny that she's weak. The more she vents exhaustion and resentment toward Joe, the more she may be confronting her children with models for how to handle anger as well as love and loyalty. Should they be careful not to anger her, and in the process develop strategies for burying their own feelings, including perhaps sympathy for Joe? Or should they leap into battle and try to match her energy, going public with disaffection for a mother they both love and depend on? Neither choice is great, but either represents a reasonable path for a child who so far lacks resources the words to express distress or wishes, the community to go to when the house swirls with conflict, or the autonomy to shrug off parents' problems as irrelevant to them.

Transactions like these at home combine with experiences out in the world to feed children's internalization of a set of rules and conclusions. The rules, or injunctions, take the form of "shoulds" and "oughts," a moral language capable of eliciting strong feelings of shame and confusion. Jimmy's hard on Mom, Jenny may think, so I should be easy; if I get angry, then I'm bad or crazy. Siena figured out that, according to the standards of a dominant group, she was not pretty. Jimmy could not bear to sit still in school and focus on the assigned work, so he suspected he was stupid and, when he overheard his teacher recommending to his parents that he be put on medication, sick.

Each time a child accepts an attribution, a label or characterization of self, he or she is also adopting a strategy, which may well be the best strategy available at the time for handling an impossible situation. Jenny may have really wanted to be helpful but found herself facing mission impossible. If she believed herself to be somehow crazed, she was allowed a safety valve. Over time, however, being resourceful, she may have found ways to suppress her anger, a greater loss of self.

Siena's conclusion that she stood outside the range of "prettiness" also took her outside the territory of "normal." Norms tend strongly to reflect characteristics of those who represent a socially dominant group. As a Jewish child in a Christian community, I felt some relief in concluding that definitions of beauty somehow had nothing to do with me; with my dark curly hair, large hips, and nose, I was simply too far off the norm. To conclude that beauty was not an option freed me to find my power as a "smart kid." There was pain involved but also satisfaction. As I grew older, I had to contend with the idea that "smart, not pretty" made me something less than feminine. It was only years later that I understood the anti-Semitism I had internalized. But at the time, the way I'd constructed my relationship to the mainstream offered redeeming features, such as a (relative) retreat from competitiveness and entry into a world of books.

In this way—by negotiating power and discovering strategies for well-being—all children learn how to be members of their social group. In Siena's class, while Siena was struggling with her sense of self, white children were simultaneously learning lessons from the other side of the mirror. In a book called *Why Are All the Black Kids Sitting in the Cafeteria Together?*, Beverly Daniels Tatum, an African-American psychologist, traces out stages in the development of racial identity. One transaction she describes is a white mother in the grocery store wheeling a child in her cart. The kid says, "Look, Mommy, why is that kid's hair so curly?"

"Ssshh," says the mom. "That's not polite." And she goes on past the black child smiling sheepishly.

What the white child learns is not to ask, that questions of racial difference are for some reason forbidden. What else, I wonder, gets lost in the process of transforming an innocent recognition of difference into a thing of danger? What other questions does the child, having not asked, end up construing as somehow laden with unacknowledged meaning? What does the child conclude about her own "normality," setting the stage for unawareness of power differentials later in life?

Out in the world by herself, Siena is beginning to absorb a whole world of social significance, as is every other child, whether of a dominant culture or a subordinated one. Where a vacuum of information exists, we all fill in blanks with our best guesses. Lacking thoughtful intervention from the grown ups around them, both white children and children of color grasp the predominance of positive images of white people and draw conclusions.

Siena's teacher is proving unable to counter that process. Over time, she seems to be developing a certain estrangement from the little girl. Not able to figure out why Siena seems sad and distant in her class, she gradually stops approaching her and looks away rather than making the effort to engage her in group activities. Perhaps she began the year by Rescuing, trying harder than proved fruitful. Now she is recognizing her own ineffectiveness, charging herself guiltily with a lack of skill (thereby casting herself as Victim). At the same time, she resents being in that position and Persecutes Siena, feeling impatience with what she sees as the child's inapproachability. The teacher does not see herself as racist; indeed, she is not intentionally so. Racism lies in her failure of imagination. Nothing in her own experience links with Siena's, and so she cannot empathize with the child's experience.

Eventually, Simone determines to move Siena into a school that is majority staff and students of color, even though it may mean less good academic resources in a poorer neighborhood.

Very often, parents of color are intensely aware of how their children are confronting issues of race and culture. But white parents rarely see the same process going on with their children. "My child has all sorts of friends," a parent might insist. "There are no issues of race." But when their kids become teenagers and confront the separation phenomenon

Tatum describes and most high school students immediately recognize ("Why *are* all the black kids sitting together in the cafeteria?"), their earlier contacts with friends of color fail to inform them of the causes. Instead, they react with surprise, hurt, and eventually hostility, seeing themselves as shunned.

The kids of color may be banding together out of a sense of ease and comfort. Unbeknownst to their white friends of a younger period, they've been wrestling with a troubling world for years, since Siena's age. Now, the "black table" in the cafeteria gives them an opportunity to develop a positive racial identity, to feel out how they fit with peers. Their separateness from white classmates may not be heavily charged emotionally. But because the white kids don't understand it, they may imbue it with more permanence and impenetrability than is inevitable. For them, it may represent loss, not only of friendships but also of the privilege of seeing themselves in the center of their social world. Commonly, white teenagers experience this phenomenon as victimization. Now, for the first time, high schoolers are confronting something they believe to be unjust that is racially based. They cannot see their own role in the process, believing all the action to lie on the other side of the color line. And so the breach grows larger over time until dynamics of race do, in fact, become intractable.

I've focused on racial dynamics to illustrate the process of internalizing models of the social world for two reasons: it is usually an area so front-and-center for parents of color and so invisible to white parents. But it is far from the only aspect of society that is acting to shape the development of both children and parents. Gender is also being shaped in ways that are very evident to most parents.

A lot of research shows that boys tend to embrace the world through movement in the early years, while girls are able sooner to learn through more sedentary means. Putting little boys in classrooms where they are enjoined to sit still, not talk out of turn, perform small motor tasks, and generally conform to methods enforced by (mostly) female teachers whose jobs depend on their ability to keep noise levels minimal, is a set up for eliciting energetic rebellion and, perhaps, along with it a less than positive self-image. Girls of this age, on the other hand, begin to experience second-class attention, because so much of teacher's energy goes to classroom discipline. When at last boys begin to participate in class activities, teacher may be so relieved she quickly calls on them, again slighting girls' primacy. Girls may figure out that their best strategy is to be "good," which is to say not to make demands on the teacher that she cannot meet. Resignation and passivity may be undercurrents of the discovery.

However much parents may try to rear non-gendered children, in all these ways and more, society contradicts the effort. Not only through images and cultural artifacts—toys and games and TV programs—but also through these daily lived experiences, gender lessons are taught and learned. While making decisions about how to handle conflict between their parents, for instance, Jenny and Jimmy were also playing with ways to be male and female. Aggression and passivity played out in their observations of the parents, paralleling dynamics between the two children. Gender often interacts with birth order; which child teases or brutalizes or which complains and fights back or submits is determined by and in turn determines complexities of femaleness and maleness later in life.

Before going on to suggest some alternative ways to deal with these matters, I want to add one more layer to the emotional experience of parents. All these events with our own children evoke our own experiences. School itself can be challenging to parents. The first time I walked into an elementary school with Tuhin, I had to discipline myself sternly to keep from grabbing him by the hand and fleeing (either screaming or giggling, I wasn't sure which) from the building. This school was little like the primary school I attended. This one was bright and colorful, experimental and friendly. Mine was an overcrowded affair of the 1940s, staffed by authoritarian teachers worn out from Depression and

War years. We were made to sit in stiff rows, without speaking to each other except at very brief recesses. Even lunch was a time of strict silence, punitively patrolled by teachers.

Some people, of course, have very warm feelings about their schooling, and they tend to cast those experiences as optimistic shadows on their children's. That's certainly a better state of mind to bring to the matter, but it is nonetheless anticipating something that might or might not be true now, and thereby communicating to children that they are somehow wrong if they aren't having the same experience.

This business of separating my experience of long ago from Tuhin's now required passage through a profound developmental stage. Earlier, I had learned to mistrust my own assumptions and learn instead from the baby. Now I had to do that on an even more difficult level. I had no recollection of my own infanthood, at least none that passed into verbal memory. But boy, did I remember kindergarten! And so it was harder to recognize that this was a different time and a different school and a different child.

Another way of viewing this parental challenge is in terms of the internalized oppression we carry within ourselves. In a sense, we are three people dealing with our children: our own most authentic selves, our mindful and skillful selves, and our socialized judgmental selves. This last facet of psyche is often the most dominating, and also the hardest to see in oneself. It is a psychological form that culture takes, which is so thoroughly internalized as to be invisible. Ideas once learned appear to be incontestable truths, common sense, beyond questioning. To see your own internalized assumptions, values, beliefs, and therefore to be able to manage your own horrors and fears and projections, is a central project for this (and every!) phase of parenting.

negotiating the outside world with awareness

The first piece of advice I offer is to be talking, as often as you can, with other people about parenting on this very personal but (you'll discover) very shared level. It is in dialogue with others that we stand the best chance of critiquing and changing our own internalizations.

My second piece of advice harkens back to my suggestion about parenting infants: listen and learn.

Earlier in the book, I've noted some forms of support on a structural level: co-housing, coops, community in a variety of shapes. Simply belonging to certain groups, however, may still not give you the kind of honest reflection I think we all need, especially when parenting. By "honest reflection" I mean being able to talk openly about your concerns and feelings, as well as being in the presence of other people doing the same thing. Therapy groups may provide such an opportunity, but I'm a firm believer in the possibility—and the advisability—of peer support that is well integrated into life. I don't think we need to rely on professional intervention to build the kind of honest dialogue that's needed.

Think of it in terms of the water metaphor: we can't see the medium in which we swim. For each of us, consciousness is limited by the judgments and assumptions we've learned along the way. If we can become aware of what those limitations are, we can challenge them. I find the concept of internalized oppression to be helpful precisely because it is about ideas we've learned. Anything learned can be challenged and changed. To be sure, these particular kinds of ideas have fierce emotional consequence, so it's often hard to find the idea underlying the feeling. Talking with others is a way to do that. For one thing, if you hear someone else speak about her own self-doubts and shortcomings, you're very likely to be unconvinced. I think people bent on mutual support mostly see the best in each other. If you can see that other person's self-image as obviously flawed, it becomes a little harder to maintain the conviction that your own internalized oppression is true.

Just as your five-year-old (and up) is learning to engage new groups of people and in the process to form new ideas about her or his self, so too do you need to be negotiating a similar developmental leap. For you, that might take the form of talking openly and regularly with a friend, or, better still, several friends. It might mean organizing a more formal peer support group. It might mean joining a group of parents at your child's school for diversity training. Or you could start a conversation with your aunt or grandmother, to go more deeply into some of your family's myths and histories.

Whatever you do is in the service of having a means to think through your work as parent, and to learn more about yourself as a social creature so that you can better guide your child through that terrain.

That brings me to my second piece of advice, about how to engage the process your child is going through. If what I've described so far seems overwhelming, rest assured that there is help available. What I'm suggesting is a partnership with your youngster.

In general, I believe people, large and small, speak the truth in whatever ways they can manage. If a child seems unhappy, tells "stories," complains of improbable things, try to err on the side of believing that something's up. With limited communication skills, the child may speak in parable or metaphor. Your job is to hear and decode the information. If you think the child is "telling stories," ask yourself why; how does the child's context give meaning and truth to what may seem to you to be lies? Something real and important is going on for the child, and your job is either to figure out a translation into terms you understand, or to ask the child to translate.

Secondly, whatever happens, talk about it. The response Tatum suggests to the grocery store example is something like, "Yes, darling, people's hair comes in all sorts of shapes and colors. Isn't that little boy's hair wonderful? He's African American, and you're (fill in the blank) and so you have very different kinds of hair."

You might also comment that pointing and staring can make other people uncomfortable: "How would it feel to you?," suggesting an empathic leap. But the heart of the observation is very worthy and deserves an honest engagement.

I think in terms of demystification. Children (very like adults) can handle most things they can identify and explain. What causes experiences like the ones I've described to be internalized as judgments is mystification. If we lie to children ("Oh, no, sweetheart, that child is just like you!"), we contradict their intuitive take on the world and undermine their sense of self and external reality.

Balancing and negotiating identities, it turns out, is a task both you and your child are encountering at this stage of life. For you, it's about home and work. For the child, it's about "who am I when I'm not at home?" Exploring this terrain in partnership gives you both some portion of the support you need in order to stay upright throughout.

5

letting go while holding tight:
the middle years

Something dramatic happened when Tuhin and, later, Josh turned seven. True, there were many distinct and wondrous transitions along the way to that point; some of the time they seemed to occur weekly.

But at seven I could sense that the kids had passed into a stage of autonomy qualitatively different from all the many steps leading up to that moment. It was not so much that I noted changes in them as that I felt a change in me. I worried less, and about very different things. It happened first with Tuhin; when he was off in the world without me, I was no longer flooded with images of this wee vulnerable leaf adrift in a stormy ocean. He was still on my mind and in my heart constantly, but the cords tying us together had suddenly become a whole lot longer.

Addressing the middle years, say between the ages of seven and fourteen, would seem a difficult task. The issues that exist at seven contrast starkly with issues confronting the parents of fourteen-year-olds. At fourteen, we're talking puberty, high school, attitude, and drugs. At seven, kids are still kids and are still dealing with play and allowances and needing to be carted around to sports events and birthday parties. But what forms a unifying framework around the whole period is the developmental task facing parents: simultaneously guiding the child through a maze of social injunctions and pressures and while assertively engaged in that protective maneuver, bit by bit, also letting the child go.

life after babies

Don't misunderstand: children remain a focus of life during this period. But they are no longer an occupation. For many years—at least seven, or more if you have more than one child—the physical needs of dependant kids have taken precedence over everything else. Now, kids are still a major influence. At home, their energy, homework, conflicts with you and with each other, set the tone, and shape your relationships with adults.

But they don't need nearly as much from you. Commonly, work in therapy shifts at this point. Latency, a term meant by developmental psychologists to suggest that not much is changing for kids (a misguided view, I believe), often marks a period of very active changes happening in parents' lives. Instead of asking, "Am I a good parent? Is my kid all right? What do I do when my four-year-old has a temper tantrum in the grocery store?," people begin to ask. "What's missing from my life?" Three questions arise again and again:

- "Do I love my partner any more?" And the corollary: "Does s/he love me?"
- "What is the meaning of this job? Am I meant to accomplish something more?"
- "What's become of the friends I had in college? Where is my community?"

Taken together, these questions describe what some folks might call a spiritual awakening. The intensity of love and labor involved in caring for young children fill life to the brim. Constant love, emotion, connection with other human beings, those and all the other compelling qualities of rearing young children may be wearing but they are also supremely satisfying. Parents hardly have time to question the meaning and purpose of their lives; there's always a child saying, "I need....," "I feel...," "I love...."

Connections with other adults may also be more plentiful. Playgrounds and childcare venues bring grown ups together. Learning on the job, parents have at least these sources of conversation. How often I've heard childless adults bemoan the loss of brain cells in their erstwhile good friends. "All she can talk about is the baby! All right already, the kid's great, but interesting? I don't think so!"

Erik Erikson, the father of developmental psychology, described the challenges facing kids at different stages as "crises." I've always doubted the accuracy of that word. Sometimes, it's true, children move from one stage to another with some degree of disquiet. But as often, the challenges they face are about new learning made possible by new physical capabilities. There is as much joy as distress in that.

But for parents at this stage, crisis may be a more apt description. Questions about spousal love often translate into matters of Rescue: less "Do we love each other?" than "Are we so burned out that we've lost the energy to find each other?" This is the time when people decide to renovate their house. "The kids are getting bigger; we'd better add that second story we've always talked about." Statistics show more divorce happens during home renovation than any other times. (I made that up, but based on anecdotal evidence, I wouldn't be surprised if it were true.) People notice that the desert of their sex lives is not simply about exhaustion. People move to another town. (This is when the Simmons moved.) They consider a love affair.

Spurred by a sense of impending disaster, couples seek counseling and/or join a church. Or they begin to act to change the world around them.

I told my mother what I was writing in this chapter, and she said, "Not me! Oh no, none of that happened to me."

"Well, wait a minute," I said consideringly. "Let's just stop and figure out what was going on when Rick (the youngest of us sibs) turned seven."

We'd moved from New York to Texas fifteen months before. It was the 1950s and the civil rights movement was building momentum. The year Rick turned seven, my parents became actively involved in progressive Democratic Party politics. My mother, until then the very definition of a homebody, ran for the school board. My father integrated his medical practice.

"You came up for air and moved out into the world big-time!" I exclaimed.

"I guess I did," said my mother, revising her story.

The route my parents took was carved out of a particular moment in history. My mother's political activism sprang from her concentration on parenting, joined with dramatic social change going on around her. (Her campaign speech started, "I have three reasons to run for the school board: Nan, Beth, Rick.")

As I write, our country lacks a social movement of the proportions of the civil rights movement. But there is plenty to be done out there, and many people already in motion to get it done. I classify social activism right up there with religion and romance as the heart of the human condition. All three flow from the human capacity--and need—for meaningful connection.

Which leads to the second realm of reassessment parents often make at this stage. Love and work, said the wise one, are what make life worthwhile. I'd add "meaningful" before "work." One of the modern world's most debilitating contributions has been the creation of alienated work. By that I mean that we work at tasks which have no integrity in our lives. We don't get to see a process through from seed to table. If we manufacture things, we mostly handle, day after day, a cog or a widget. More of us these days work in service industries. We answer telephones, file papers, and email endlessly. And somewhere along the way we lose clarity about why we're doing all of that. People in the social services begin to feel like hamsters on the wheel, always running, never getting anywhere. All that for only a paycheck? That way lies bondage!

Only a privileged few actually get to work with the people they want, doing what they want, feeling gratified by the results. For more, the existential questions--"What's it all about? Is this what I was put on earth for?"—loom darkly on the horizon.

All right, I don't want to overdo it. I mean to suggest that once your kids are no longer so entirely dependant, you have the space as well as the need to evaluate your own life. It has by now become clear that parenting is a transitory occupation. Amazingly, your kids *will* grow up and move out. They may not be there yet, but they've proven the principle. Among the many headaches modernity gives us, it also provides longevity. In all probability, you'll have many years beyond parenting: what are they for?

All the more reason to ensure that you have rich relationships surrounding you. Community, or the lack thereof, may become starkly problematic at this stage. It's the third "crisis" I hear in therapy, although not many people are fully aware that that's what they lack. We are so socialized to individualism, to the belief that we should be all we need alone, or at most in a couple, that many of us lack enough vision of community even to mourn its absence. Individualism, carried to the extremes of American culture, is a prime example of internalized oppression. We are as much fundamentally social beings as we are existentially alone. Yet the water of beliefs and values in which we swim dramatically tilts us toward the alone side of that duality. As the ties with children lengthen, the need for more human connection becomes apparent on a spiritual level rather than a practical one. Before, we needed help; now, we need companionship.

Take care of yourself. Honor your own dissatisfactions as much as you've learned to honor your child's. Take inspiration from watching your kids moving on: you, too, deserve the joy of experiencing the next stage in your own life.

Thankfully, that goal is also good parenting, indeed precisely what you should be doing right now for the sake of your kids. The richer your own life is, the better you can measure and negotiate your relationship with them. Show up for your children because it's what they need, not because it's what *you* need. What better modeling can you give them than the example of you working toward well-being in your own life?

For parenting itself is far from over. Just as you (hopefully!) learned in romantic relationships, so now too the goal is to accomplish an intricate, confusing, skill-demanding dance between poles of intimacy and autonomy. Well danced, the equation becomes a whole lot less tension-filled in the remaining years that kids live at home, the dreaded years of adolescence. Maybe it's idealistic, but I can see fun and love ahead for you and your teenager.

negotiating extracurricular activities

One of the most prominent ways middle class parents are still involved with kids happens in the car.

How many hours do you spend transporting children from one place to another? Lessons, sports, tutoring, clubs, all occur at distances, small or great. Rare is the middle class child these days who doesn't need a secretary to keep track of all her or his commitments.

Kelly is the stay-at-home mom of a blended family of seven. At least, she wishes she could stay at home. Kurt, her husband, is an overworked physician. His hours pretty much prohibit his donning the chauffeur's cap. Every morning, Kelly takes five children to three different schools. (The two oldest thankfully take the bus.) She picks them up at four different times in the afternoon. There's not an afternoon when she doesn't hit at least five after-school locations, between different soccer teams, music lessons, Ashley's drama club, not to mention the occasional dentist or doctor's appointment. Much of that time, she has tired, squabbling kids in the car for company.

Little wonder that by the time Kelly does truly get home, just in

time to start cooking dinner, she's fried. Patience is a dimly remembered place she visited once-upon-a-time in the past. Her step-kids act
as if they hate her; her own two are jealous of any evening time she
doesn't spend with them. Much as she cares for Kurt, she's wondering
what ever possessed her to remarry. She remembers the executive career she'd been so happy to leave then with warm nostalgia now.

Kelly's plight may be the extreme end of the spectrum. But the
wear and tear on parents of over-committed urban and suburban kids
is one of the most frequent complaints I hear. Car pools help, but they
take management skills which are themselves tiring. In "the good old
days," when Tuhin and Josh each turned seven, I could introduce them
to the public bus system and turn them loose. Inner city kids may still
travel that way. But middle class parents often fear the dangers of an
impersonal and violent society, and so they trade the constant drain of
driving for the protection of the private automobile.

How much more sane everyone's lives would be if we truly focused
on child safety. Imagine a system of buses supervised by effective adult
monitors during the hours when kids are apt to travel. Perhaps there
could even be under-eighteen-only transit. Massive community watch
programs could make our streets safe for children again. Or even a
genuine return to the beat cop would help, adequately supported and
in adequate numbers, people who knew the kids of a community and
focused on protecting them. Structures like these would support developmental progress for both kids and adults: more autonomy, more
mobility, less grouchiness all around.

Idealistic, you think? I don't. It's a matter of policy, which is a matter
of priorities. Public officials speak endlessly these days of values-based
politics. But the values implied do little for children and the adults who
care for them. I'm not sure what percentage of the electorate is parenting as I write, but I'd bet as a unified voting bloc it would be significant,
especially on the local level where children's lives play out. Here's the
catch twenty-two, however: you might need to stop all that driving

around in order to have time to organize politically. On the other hand, cell phone technology might be just the ticket!

The other side of the extra-curricular conundrum is one positive impact on parents' lives. Peter has for years bemoaned the thinness of community life for his family. Now that his older boy Phil plays basketball, though, Peter has a new sense of connection. A group of team parents sit together at practices and games. They band together to take kids to out-of-town matches. They coordinate bringing refreshments, and they politic about selecting coaches and funding equipment. Peter loves it; it's become his world every bit as much as his son's.

But there's a problem implicit in the gift of community. Phil's thinking of quitting the team. He's tired of how much time it takes; he'd much rather spend that time playing a new generation of computer games he's just discovered. Oh yeah, and he might also use some of the time for homework. Peter keeps making arguments about the value of sport: Phil needs exercise. The computer is a sinkhole just waiting to devour him. All those critiques have truth to them, but the underlying deal—that Peter would miss the companionship of the other parents—fuels a steely intransigence by the father that is increasingly fomenting the son's rebelliousness.

Eventually, Peter gives in. He knows when he's beat. And besides, he realizes Phil would outgrow basketball some day anyhow. He can't rely on his children's athletic lives to satisfy his own need for community.

Other parents get hooked into the sports scene by their competitive ambitions for their kids. We've all seen magazine stories about the cut-throat soccer mom, or a dad screaming invectives at a Little League son who's missed an easy hit. Competition is a mixed bag. On the one hand, American children will grow up to make their way in a highly competitive society. Knowing how to hold their own may be necessary. On the other hand, there's a strong element of internalized oppression involved. Choosing to compete is very different from believing one's worth resides in winning. How do we separate the two? One way is for parents to get very clear about what thread in the fabric is about their own need for credibility and success, what is about their children, and in consequence what they are communicating on an emotional as well as an articulated level. The message unsaid is the most powerful. Silence may nor may not be golden, depending on the context, but it is surely very loud.

learning "differences" and other dilemmas of diagnosis

Another important sphere in which parents' needs and feelings get mixed up with children's is around academic success. I want to preface this discussion with a personal disclosure of bias. I wrote earlier about my visceral reaction to Tuhin's school, and I chalked it up to my own grim academic beginnings. But in truth there is more to my feelings about education than that.

If there's one fact about humanity I've found proven over and over again, it is diversity. I'm not talking about five races or two (or more) genders, about two hundred nationalities or anything so finite. The range of approaches to thinking, feeling, and learning, is, I believe, enormously greater than we credit. It far, far out spans what our schools have to offer.

What a paradox that there is a growing literature by American authors detailing different kinds of intelligence. Howard Gardner's work identifying seven distinct types of intelligence is joined by David Goleman's *Emotional Intelligence*. Feminism insists that intuitive ways of knowing are as credible as linear ones, and a world of spiritual explorers laud the merits of holistic thinking.

Yet our education system moves more and more toward teaching-to-the-test, a standardization of assessment that locks teachers into standardized curricula, as if there could be a standardized form of learning. Wrong!

We try to force our children into step with one very limited modality, and then, when they don't learn, or don't behave, or otherwise tell

us that something's wrong, we resort to good old American individualism and say, "It's you who's wrong." We may try to discipline them
into line, or bribe them, or coerce them. Ultimately, when none of that
works, we diagnose them.

Celeste and Virginia have two children, one birthed by Virginia,
the other adopted. Because Virginia had always wanted to experience
pregnancy and birth, and Celeste had no such burning desire, when
they were ready for children they decided to mix their gene pools by
inviting Celeste's brother to donate sperm. The result was Anthony.

Meanwhile, not knowing whether conception would succeed, the
couple had explored a variety of ways to adopt. They looked into private adoptions in the U.S., which they found to be more costly than
they could afford. They thought about adopting a "special needs" child,
but both worked full time at careers that mattered to them so they felt
it wouldn't be right to take on a child who needed more attention than
they could provide. In the end, they opted to adopt a little girl from
Colombia and they named her Amanda.

Now the two children are eight and nine. Amanda has always been
a super-fine student. Every teacher she's had praised her to the skies, and
now that she's in grade-giving grades, she consistently gets straight As.

Anthony, on the other hand, has always struggled with school. He's
been less happy to be there, has trouble focusing on schoolwork, becomes alternately sullen and angry when his moms press him to do his
homework. At the urging of the school counselor, Celeste and Virginia
took him for testing.

It was not an easy decision. Both women questioned the wisdom of
placing a label on a child. Moreover, the process was expensive; neither
the school nor their health insurance covered the cost. Nonetheless,
desperation drove them to give it a try.

The educational therapist put Anthony through a battery of tests. In
the end, she diagnosed him as ADHD, Attention Deficit Hyperactivity
Disorder, and referred them to a psychiatrist for medication. Anthony

was put on Aderal, a drug with opposite effects on children and adults, slowing the former down, speeding the later up. Anthony complained and resisted, but his moms insisted.

The decision to put a child on medication does not come easily to most parents. There is a very fine line between behavior control through chemistry and therapeutic uses of drugs. Some three to five percent of school children in America are diagnosed ADHD and medicated, according to the National Institute of Mental Health. It is a diagnosis given to boys five to seven times more frequently than to girls. African-American children are one-and-a-half times more likely to be diagnosed learning disabled than white children. Similar disproportions hold for Latino and Native American kids. Research into long term effects of medication is lacking; the drug prescribed for Anthony was recently banned in Canada because of associations with heart disease. Another commonly prescribed drug, Cylert, is known to cause liver damage and is recommended only as a last resort. New information on many medications surfaces regularly, altering physicians' reliance on them.

I strongly favor exhausting all other approaches to the kinds of issues that get diagnosed as ADHD. Most classrooms favor a very particular kind of learning and behavior. It requires stillness, sitting with books, and drawing on small pieces of paper. Recent research on how sex hormones influence brain development tends to confirm anecdotal evidence that many boys, as I've mentioned before, have trouble before the age of seven or so doing precisely those things. It doesn't take long for a child, told to sit still when his body says "Move!" to come into conflict with a classroom setting. Anthony's teachers reported from the very beginning that he was a sweet child, wanting to please, but seeming to be incapable of doing the sedentary tasks they assigned the class. I wondered whether he might have been more typical of other boys than appeared on the surface and just reared by his mothers to express himself more fully. By the time many children enter kindergarten, they've often internalized commands to be still and cause no trouble. They may be better equipped to mask their neurological inclinations, able to adopt strategies to contain their impulses and acquiesce obediently. It's possible that Anthony's kinesthetic mode is on the high end of a range. But it's equally possible that a large element of the dynamic is social.

Nutrition, too, is seen by many practitioners to be a factor. Elements ranging from iron content in foods to amino acids, from sugars to magnesium have appeared to different researchers to be associated with ADHD. It's often difficult to regulate a bouncy boy's food intake in enough detail to make a difference, but it seems to me well worth trying.

Even more, I hear Anthony's story as a compelling cry for schoolrooms tailored to the brain and body functions of the children that they serve. If some large number of children cannot sit still, ideally we would have classrooms based on kinesthetic learning. Some children learn better visually and others learn better verbally through story-telling. If we devoted enough resources to education, we could have smaller classrooms with better funded teachers trained to understand and address the needs of their students. We might not, then, need to medicate children to make them adapt to a one-style-fits-all pedagogy.

My impression is that diagnoses change as children get older. ADHD is more an issue for younger children. By seven to fourteen, the frame for viewing pathology (and despite the nice euphemism of "learning difference," we are in fact suggesting a norm from which some individuals deviate) more often becomes learning disabilities. Interestingly, it is here that a range of differences is in fact reflected, but in terms of diagnoses. The panel of possible labels for these differences grows steadily longer as a field of educational therapy takes shape. Educational therapists often use these concepts and diagnoses as entry points to working with children in wonderfully supportive ways. A child who, like Anthony, has experienced himself or herself as a mysteriously "wrong" learner is often relieved to have a name for what ails him, even if the name compounds the individualism error. Resources become available, in the form of help from a savvy teacher who gets to work one-to-one with the child, forming a warm and responsive mutual relationship. Occasionally there's even public money available to pay for the intervention.

Why can't we fund schools adequately so that every child gets the benefit of such individualized attention? Imagine classrooms with a teacher/student ratio of four. Perhaps they'd have fluid walls, so students could flow in and out of relationship with many different children and adults throughout the day. Years ago, when my children were young, I fantasized a utopian learning environment: a community in which adults worked close to home and children flowed in and out of the offices and workshops and farms of their elders. There would be "guides" to support kids in finding the knowledge they desired and needed based on their interests and talents. Eventually, children would learn the basic skills, not because they were made to sit down with dry books, but because they wanted to know how to measure wood in order to make a toy or how plants germinate so they could grow a flower garden.

I still entertain that utopian fantasy. How satisfying it would be for grown-ups as well as kids!

As your children get older, the cultural ethers continue to be inhabited by these hard issues. By the time kids reach the teen years, depression has become a common diagnosis, although it is being applied to children of younger and younger ages as time goes on. Looking at it through a social rather than a medical lens, I cannot but ask what is making so many children sad? How understandable it is that children might become depressed if they have been forced to be a way not natural to them many hours each day . I think of depression as alienation, separation from ones self as well as from others. Ill suited educational systems alienate children, and, lo and behold!, they become symptomatic.

Very, very rarely, a child's symptom might be the product of some neurological or physiological phenomenon unconnected with the experiences of daily life. But far more often I believe that we acknowledge, hyperactivity, depression, and other frequently-diagnosed feeling states as expressions of distress or reactions to something problematic going on around the person. Here again, I believe the responsibility of adults is to pay attention, to learn to translate the language of children into useful words, and to move toward pathology as an explanation only when every other option has been exhausted.

At the same time, I know how hard it is to find or create the resources that your child needs. Even while I urge you to try, I also want to encourage you to see the problem as one of policy and public choices, not as your failure as a parent any more than you would if your child came down with chicken pox.

One nine-year-old girl I worked with was a dreamer living in a family of high academic and professional achievers. At home, surrounded by two very verbal older sisters, a very verbal younger brother, and two very verbal parents, Cornelia rarely spoke. Her parents brought her to me for assessment for anti-depressants.

I asked her whether she had any troubles she'd like to discuss, and the following conversation ensued:

Cornelia: I'm fine. I don't have any problems. Except I get afraid.

Beth: Of what?

C: Well, of the pitch dark. And sometimes I tell different people different things.

B: Which people?

C: Well, sometimes my parents.

B: Why?

C: Because they're divorced, and I sort of tell them what they want to hear.

B: What are you scared of?

C: You know, of a *[gestures back and forth with hand]*, of a commotion. I'm really different with my friends. I talk a lot with them. But at home, I don't want to cause a commotion. There's enough commotion already.

I asked Cornelia to describe "commotion." "When everyone talks at once, and they all disagree, and they end up mad at me, and I don't really know what I've done.

"So I try not to say anything, and sometimes when I do, I just make up a little story that I think they want to hear."

When her father joined us in my consultation room and posed the question about medication, Cornelia looked alarmed. "Please don't give me medicine to change my mind," she pleaded. "I like my mind!"

I liked her mind, too. I instructed her parents and siblings to treat the family scene as an exercise in multiculturalism. Everyone but my client belonged to one culture, she to another. "Study her," I suggested. "Regard her with awe. She's a stranger in your midst, and you have a lot to gain by clearing space so she can reveal herself and you can get to know her."

A year later, the father told me Cornelia had blossomed at school and was still quiet, but peaceably, acceptably quiet, at home.

Anthony, too, was the odd person out in his family. His physical energy was different. His way of learning was different. His talents and inclinations were different. In my experience, most families have at least one member who is different--not sick, not crazy, just different. Embracing that person and supporting his or her style and needs can ease tensions and enlighten everyone involved.

mean girls, bonded boys

Being the odd-person-out at home is painful; being that person at school is something else again. A problem parents have talked about increasingly over the years is that their daughter is being treated badly at school by other girls. I doubt the phenomenon is altogether new. Margaret Atwood wrote a novel on the subject, *Cat's Eye,* vividly describing similar dynamics a generation past. In my own childhood, a hundred years ago, relationships among girls may have been as thorny, but they were far more underground.

At around nine or ten, as girls reach forward toward puberty, cruel competitiveness sometimes sets in. The coin of trade is friendship. Patty shuns her best friend Susan and takes up with Cynthia, someone everyone has rejected up until then. Susan weeps and rages, provoking Patty to flaunt her rejection all the more dramatically. Susan begins to hate school; every morning she has a stomach ache and doesn't want to get out of bed. She won't tell her parents what's up, partly because she scorns their understanding, but mostly because she dreads their intervention. "They'd want to talk to the teacher," she tells me privately. "What a dork thing to do! I'd never hear the end of it."

So Susan is trapped. The harder she may try to find her way back into the center of her social group, the worse other girls treat her. Months pass, and then one day when she creeps sadly into the lunch room, Cynthia calls out, "Sit here by me, Susan!" Suddenly, she finds herself courted by Patty's erstwhile pal. Patty pouts and whispers made-up stories to other girls, but Cynthia turns a shoulder in her direction and resolutely courts Susan instead.

By this age girls have been forcefully molded toward relationship, continuing the gender traditions of yore. But they are also steeply influenced by cultural figures who break that mold: punk singer Avril Lavigne, soccer star Mia Hamm, or singer/actress Queen Latifah. They've seen their mothers and other adult women in their lives work in the world outside, and they've overheard them talk about the dramas and successes of their own competitive styles. They watched their parents sally forth in the gender wars at home, and they've noticed that their mothers demand perfection and give little quarter. They join soccer teams and are encouraged to be aggressive and to win.

On the one hand, that sweet little nine-year-old girl is attuned toward the nuances of affection and rejection; on the other, she's determined to take no hostages in pursuit of her own goals.

Out of that mix arises the phenomenon of the mean girl at school, the very same child who is the little sweetheart at home—right up until the moment when that switches, too.

Parents, meanwhile, have little clue of the dense social maelstrom their daughters are experiencing. Girls who are the targets of exclusion may become troubled, but they often won't confess to parents the reasons why. Girls who are the perpetrators of selection are less detectable still. People in a one-up power position feel and appear confident and happy; it's a failure of power that causes distress.

Boys may actually be experiencing a comparable set of dynamics. But for them they are structured and labeled through the medium of sports. Not that athletic pursuits nowadays are exclusively a male prerogative, however. But gender does tend to shape the meaning of sports differently for boys and for girls. The former receive less ambivalent messages about aggression and competitiveness. The field of play mirrors life generally rather than contradicting it. Dynamics are overtly moderated by rules of good sportsmanship, even while parents shout invectives from the sidelines. "How you play the game" is often not the point; winning is.

Team sports, in general, train participants to understand and accept rules, parameters within which to strategize accomplishment. They may also teach something about the benefit of adhering to clear-cut roles. Years ago in Little League, most of the kids wanted to pitch. Tuhin knew he was a better third-baseman than a pitcher, however, and insisted the coach privilege realism about players' capabilities over democratic process. Joshua refused to play team sports at all, preferring the free form creativity of skating and the companionship of imaginative game-playing with friends.

Parents today frequently complain about the time pressures of their children's athletic activities. "Here's what my Saturday looks like," said Dennis, the father of three children under the age of eight. "I take Simon to his baseball game on one side of town, race back to the other side to drop Judy off at soccer, and then stay with the little one at gymnastics for an hour, leaving me just enough time to go back across town to pick up Simon, sweep around again for Judy. Then, as my reward, I get to take three tired and cranky children out for pizza.

"Not exactly the day of rest I need after a week of work!"

If the developmental tasks facing parents at this stage of the process are to make conscious the messages inherent in children's lives and to adapt to their kids' ever-greater autonomy, there are many ways that sports present dilemmas: First, they tend to advance children's dependency on parents for transportation and support. Second, they sometimes hook parents into one of the few sources of community around (witness Peter above). Finally, over-extended athletic lives may give parents exaggerated power to approve and disapprove of their offspring's actions, just at a time when the judgments of peers and non-familial adults is becoming more and more important. More than once I've witnessed a mom or dad go off on a child who had just struck out or missed a soccer goal, with the result that the child turned red and teary, clearly embarrassed in front of peers and strangers. Struggling with public shaming is not, I believe, ever a positive way to teach a child anything. What it does convey is a message determinedly in the direction of some of the worst features of mainstream life in America: that the strong deserve to prevail, that weakness is sin, that winning aces relationship, and that the stick is mightier than the carrot.

All of which is not to say that organized sports are intrinsically bad. They can be done in a way that mixes a modicum of competition with a larger dose of fun and companionship. A mistaken move can be cheered, encouragement extended with kindness. Even more, team sports offer plentiful opportunities to talk about process. To point out to children what dynamics are taking place is to raise consciousness about alternatives and choice. We cannot exempt our children altogether from the forces of individualism and competitiveness in our society, but we can help them to see these dynamics for what they are, to counter notions that the child is somehow deficient or needs to prove worthiness on the field of competition.

6

all grown up with nowhere to go:
fifteen to eighteen

Developmental challenges:
1) Faith and steadiness
2) Managing terror

Now we come to the Big Scare: the Teenager! Parents joke about it:

"How badly nature organizes things. Just as the kid hits the high hormones of adolescence, Mom hits the low hormones of meno-pause!"

"How soon am I allowed to kick the miserable so-and-so out of the house?! S/he's driving me nuts!"

"I'm not ready for this. What happened to that sweet little kid who used to kiss me good-night?!"

Over and over again, parents register surprise and dismay that they suddenly find themselves living with a gangly, grumpy, disagreeable, and angry stranger.

Of all the parents who have asked me to write an advice book over the years, none is as desperate as the parent of a teenager.

My own experiences of parenting two teens were very, very differ-ent. Tuhin (and I) had the very good fortune of access to a teen-cen-tered, virtually adult-free house where he could hang out with peers most of the time. The parents of two brothers in his circle were involved in building a new home in a community fifty miles away. They trusted their boys and left them alone for long periods of time. The whole group of their friends practically lived together with autonomy.

I knew of a tribal people in India called the Muria who invited their young people to inhabit a teens-only house called a *ghotul*. Kids could move in at any age they wished. They could visit their biological families any time they chose, but their parents couldn't visit them. Adults were strictly prohibited from entering the *ghotul*. The teenagers made their own social rules, including standards of sexual conduct. Left entirely free by the tribe to create their own world, they were given only one responsibility, an important and honored one: to be the official greeters of visitors to the village.

When I'd first learned of the Muria's *ghotul,* I'd thought it was an entirely sensible way to handle the transition from childhood to adulthood that we call adolescence. Kids are safe while learning to be adult. They are granted control of contact with their elders, and they are trusted to represent the community as a whole in the important and diplomatic arena of relations with outsiders.

To me, Tuhin's friends' house seemed as close as we were going to come to the *ghotul* model. I recognized that conditions in an isolated village in India were very different from those in San Francisco in the 1980s. There had begun to be press attention to kidnappings of children on the streets (one famous one only a block from Tuhin's school). There was much alarm about gang violence and the hazards of drugs in the community.

But I trusted that the boys of Tuhin's group (they were mostly male, although with a sprinkling of girls, too) were sensible kids, especially after they volunteered to us parents that they had a sworn agreement never to be in a car with a driver who'd been drinking. In our immediate social group at that point, the only injuries and deaths of young people were vehicular in nature, so the designated driver pact was reassuring.

I asked Tuhin to call and let me know where he'd be every evening. If I expected him home late at night and he chose instead to go to his friends' house, I asked that he come home first and slip a note under the door declaring his whereabouts. I wanted to be informed but not awakened. Finally, I asked that someone answer the phone at the friends' house whenever it rang. (It was the pre-cell-phone era.)

Tuhin readily agreed and remained faithful to those agreements throughout his high school years. Whatever curtailment of independence the arrangements involved for him were more than compensated by my trusting calmness and his enormous freedom.

Tuhin was easy. He was a good student, valued by teachers and classmates at his high school. He was adept at using public transportation and neither needed nor desired chauffeuring. He was personable, knew how to win favorable attention from others, and so on.

He was also a young man of color. I had watched shop-keepers over the years track him with their eyes, even while Josh, blond-haired, blue-eyed, innocent-looking little angel, pocketed small, enchanting items from the five and dime. (Unlike Tuhin, Joshua wasn't much interested in money for its own sake and had a hard time accepting the idea of commercial transaction.) Many of Tuhin's friends were African-American; he identified culturally and racially with them, based on how he was seen by the larger world rather than his genetic origins.

So I did live with a certain amount of anxiety about his well-being. My willingness to turn him loose was advanced by help and support from people in my larger community. Becky's father, for instance, was a labor organizer. He'd worked in his younger days as a longshore-man. He was without illusion about the rough-and-tumble world of men in the city. When the boys' were young he'd begun a conversation with them about street smarts, and he'd convinced us moms that the children's best protection was knowing what to expect, combined with strategies for taking care of themselves.

Josh was a very different sort of kid. He'd never found the kind of notice for his talents Tuhin had. He was quiet in school, living an interior life that was rich and imaginative but not visible to those who weren't looking for it—and most public school teachers had little time or energy to seek out the less obvious wonders of their thirty or so students. Early on, Josh discovered the joy of drumming. He was a natural musician of enormous talent. We turned the garage into a (reasonably) sound-proofed studio, and Josh's social circle expanded from kids in the neighborhood to kids in the band. But his music rarely made its way into visibility at school. His renown was real but reached a limited audience.

Tuhin went on from high school to college. Josh dropped out of high school. He was sexually active early on—and, I might add, found popularity with girls he had never enjoyed with teachers. Where Tuhin embarked on a well-charted path (with, nonetheless, some troubling twists and turns), Joshua had to create his own. His teen years were filled with some of the horrors that visit parents in the night: sex, drugs, and rock-and-roll.

But somehow both boys survived--and so did we parents. For us, it wasn't always a fun ride, although there were times of joy and love and growth as well as fear and pain. Over all, it tested our belief in our kids and our reliance on each other, and, in long retrospect, I think we all came out the better for it.

demons and angels

We live in a society that teaches us well how to compete for control, how to take power and hold onto it. What we're not taught, though, is how to give up power and control. I'm not talking about being overcome or ceding needed ground, but about handing control to its rightful owner. That is the developmental lesson we stand to learn from our teenagers. As kids acquire size and mobility, they stretch and grasp for greater independence. Quite naturally, they want to test their wings, to fall a few times with (hopefully) soft landings and to learn thereby their own lessons. They want to grow steadily stronger, more capable of making their own decisions, and more autonomous.

At precisely this time, kids' exposure to danger grows measurably greater. Out alone in the great world, they are subject to hazards that parents may so far have worked to protect *them* from with a fair measure of success. The dilemma facing parents, therefore, is not a new one: how to hand over power measure by measure, to guide rather than control, and to assess risks. What is new is the strength of force on the other side of that process. You may be cautiously, judiciously loosening your grip on the reins, but meanwhile your teenager is likely to be yanking for all s/he's worth. Moreover, the force s/he exerts is probably not constant. Exactly when you're prepared to hold on tight, the rope goes slack. You look up amazed to find a fun and affectionate young one draped around your neck. This was the point at which Tuhin put his arm sweetly around my shoulder and said, "Mom, you know I love you. I just don't want to hang out with you right now."

But then, just when you think adolescence is all right after all, suddenly you find yourself nose to nose with a snarling kid fighting over some (to you) minor point as if for life itself. Your new tasks are to expect the unexpected and to accept the growing limitations to your ability to act.

If that's not enough to set your heart to quaking, just to get them out in the open, here's a list of the things parents of teenagers tell me they most fear:

- violence either at the hands of other teens or of police, either on the streets or in automobiles
- rape and other forms of sexual assault
- suicide, or the lesser forms of depression
- substance abuse
- failure to succeed at school
- collapse of relationships at home

Violence is a concern disproportionately affecting parents of girls of all races and African-American and Hispanic boys. In white suburbs, people may be as alarmed by violence and as protective of their sons as are people in the inner city. But statistically, their vulnerability is far less real. We have two fundamental sources of information about issues like this one: first-hand experience and second-hand cultural products. In the latter category are the evening news, the local newspaper, movies, TV generally – that is, a media saturated with stories of disaster and alarm. Some proportion of the story presented is exaggerated for the purpose of selling products; some is not. How are you to keep the balance? Direct experience, usually a reliable guide, may not help much in this context. "I can't believe how many risks I took when I was her/his age!" parents frequently exclaim. "I got by OK, but I'm terrified for her/him!" She or he is not you, nor are the times the same.

"It's a really different world," I hear people say all the time. "Neighbors, shopkeepers, all adults watched out for us when we were coming up. But now, nobody knows my kids, nobody cares." Some of that nostalgia may be over-blown, more a product of myth and wish than fact. But in general, today's families do inhabit worlds that are more alienated from community than parents' worlds were. That reality translates easily into a sense of mystification. What is it really like out there for them? We were experimenting with pot; what are they being exposed to? How altered is their judgment by peer pressure?

Not knowing equals not being in control, adding another layer to the physical limitations of parents' powers. Time spent together is less than before. Friends may be strangers to parents, unknown in their immediate social circle. Anxiety runs deep and wide, and many parents do something altogether understandable but largely mistaken: they try harder and harder to exert control. To their surprise, their teenagers react rebelliously. They become walled off, hostile, intent on nothing so much as asserting their independence. Their judgment does indeed become skewed, because their attention is focused on the hazard they perceive at home—being held captive—not on potential danger out in the world.

For parents to do the opposite of tightening control, letting go more and more rather than pulling back on the reins with hard, panicked jerks, runs counter both to emotions and to training. "What are my responsibilities here?" parents often ask, voices inflected by thick mixtures of fear, anger, and doubt. This is a time when dynamics of Rescue come to dramatic climax. Children who have been treated as less responsible and able than they may have been at an earlier time, now, aware that they inhabit adult-sized bodies and thick teenage peer communities, suddenly assert themselves as adult. They move from Victim role to Persecutor, big time. Indeed, often the energy of that shift is accelerated by all the passion of childhood funneled into declarations of independence. "I want to be trusted," becomes, "I want to be left strictly alone to do whatever I please." Faced with the realities of being left strictly alone, however, kids suddenly feel aggrieved that parents are not driving them places, giving them sizeable allowances, buying them fashions, washing their clothes, and so on. Child states alternate with adult ones in bewildering rapidity, and parents flail about trying to find some footing, a firm place from which to exercise parental responsibility and authority, even as they see the latter increasingly challenged.

These are the moments when Angelica turns into Demonica. Wild girls are a particular feature of modern adolescence. I'm struck by how many parents work in therapy on their shock and dismay about sweet daughters who seem suddenly to become angry hellions. I wrote in the last chapter about ways these twelve- and thirteen-year-olds are registering hard transitions in our social definitions of femininity. Chosen models today are more likely to be tough, capable, self-determined heroines than the domestic helpmates or passive sexual objects of their parents' generation. Beyond cultural archetypes, today's girls experience the adult women in their lives as strong. They work, they fight with their partners, they get noticed in the world. For the most part, immediate adult female models demonstrate activism rather than obedience. Yet young girls are still inundated with messages about taking second place, waiting to be asked, and being helpful and caring and kind. Mothers may be experiencing comparable contradictions and handling them by mammoth quantities of overwork. These Rescues show up as angry exchanges with others in the family, so daughters equate female responsibility with a bad temper. The contradictions chafe and girls react rebelliously.

The closer kids, both boys and girls, come to leaving home, the more intense grow the dynamics.

getting ready to depart

"I'm eighteen!" Adam had just been released from a day in the psychiatric ward after swallowing a bunch of pills. "Can't you just leave me alone!?"

The only child of a single mom, Adam was declaring himself adult in no uncertain, yet highly problematic, terms. His mother had called me a few days before his suicide attempt, wanting help mediating her rocky relationship with him.

"He's smoking dope and suddenly failing things at school, even though he's only two months away from graduating. I don't know what to do!" she'd cried on the phone.

Every parent's worst fear? Drugs and school failure, insubordination and suicide: Adam was presenting his mother with it all.

I talked with Adam alone the day after his release from the hospital. "I didn't really mean to die," he said. "I just felt hopeless. My mom is so controlling, she just won't give up."

Through an extensive evaluation, a variety of things convinced me he wasn't in further danger of suicide. I thought he was less a depressed young man than a really angry one.

Bearded, with long curly hair, Adam sat with his face barely visible behind the hirsute veil. But when I said, "You know, that's often the deal at this point in a kid's life: you want to be treated as an adult, and your mom's not ready. She's scared. Also, you still depend on her for things like financial support, and also I imagine for other kinds of things, like belief in you. So you're both kind of stuck, yes?"

Adam looked up through his curls with a half-smile. "Guess so," he agreed. His clear blue eyes gleamed with understanding.

"Are you up for some negotiation of terms?" I asked.

"Guess so," he agreed and with a decided gesture swept a clump of tangled hair behind his ear.

Adam and his mother, Bettina, had long been close to each other. Bettina really enjoyed parenting in general and parenting Adam in particular. An artist, she had a grand capacity for play and for love. I could sense the foundation that connection had laid down in Adam; he was a young man as capable of reflection as he was of passionate and impulsive acts like swallowing a fistful of pills.

They came to see me together a few days later. Before we began the conversation, I asked Adam to make a commitment both to his mother and to me that he would not attempt suicide again. The threat of self-inflicted death, indeed of any bodily harm, so far imbalances a relationship that it makes cooperative problem-solving impossible. If Bettina feared that Adam might kill himself, she would be very likely to walk on egg shells, to keep silent about her own feelings and needs: in short, to Rescue with the problematic consequences we've already visited. Adam made the commitment and talked movingly about the moment of despair he'd felt when he'd done it. So much of it grew from his sense that his mother was fighting him in his determination to be independent, that he had no power to get her to do what she'd always before done: support and nurture his goals. Now, however, he knew he didn't want to die. The suicidal act had made things worse, and he had no intention of, nor could he imagine, ever doing anything like it again. Nonetheless, together we framed a plan for what he'd do instead, should he ever be in that kind of despair again.

That done, I turned to Bettina and asked her to talk about how she was feeling in the aftermath of the suicide attempt and Adam's statement. She looked at her hands clenched in her lap, and for a long, long beat was silent. Finally, she drew a breath, looked up, tears streaming from her eyes. "I was so frightened," she whispered. "Adam, I love you more than anything in life. I was so scared I'd lose you."

Adam said nothing, but his eyes moistened, too. I felt the connection flicker back into life between them, and I invited them to go on, honestly to clear the air by giving respectful voice to the trouble they were having with each other.

This procedure of speaking emotional truths we've encountered before in the book. I've written in an earlier chapter about a nuanced relationship between power and honesty, and that theme shows up in dialogue between parents and children as an asymmetry in emotional dialogue. A parent will always be a parent. However adult a child may be, mom or dad's voice carries influence that is increased by the nature of their historic relationship, as well as by the realities of the present. As Adam and his mother talked, they crossed some subtle lines of silence. Both encouraged and constrained by my presence, guided by my counsel to speak respectfully but truthfully, Adam opened out, talking in simple language about his perceived hardships.

First, he grieved his mother's insistence on a curfew, next her attempts to control his homework, and finally her suspicions and rules about drugs. Bettina's complaints suggested a matching set of experiences: he wouldn't talk to her and he moped around the house, silent and hostile. She expressed wonderment and anxiety about his declared intention to drop out of school two months before graduation. She connected his failures at school with his marijuana use.

Once they'd exhausted their lists of troubles, I talked about the transition they were negotiating. The end of high school is both a joyous thing and a frightening one. For some youths, the next steps are mapped out in reassuring security: college, maybe part-time jobs, living in the semi-protection of a dorm, at least for the first year away from home. That prototypic journey, however, is only real for a minority of new high school graduates. Adam had been accepted to a state university, so he had the option of going or not. But many young people lack the financial resources or the interest to be full-time college students.

Instead, they go directly into the workforce, sometimes combining new jobs with part-time courses at the local community college.

Adam had decided he wanted to bypass the transitional guardianship of full-time college for the greater autonomy offered by a job. "Anything!" he declared with vigor. "I'm willing to do anything to get away on my own."

"McDonalds?" I asked. "How about helper on a construction site?"

"Well, maybe not anything."

But it turned out that Adam had been talking with friends of the family and people in the neighborhood about jobs, and he did in fact have some credible leads. I suggested he work up a plan, including research on how much share-rentals were going for, how much his expenses beyond rent would run, what he was thinking of doing about health insurance, all in the context of what level of salary was offered by the jobs he was considering. In other words, I supported his choices and at the same time encouraged him to take the responsibility for realism that goes along with the power he sought.

Bettina, meanwhile, was squirming in her chair. "Pretty scary, huh?" I commented. "The task facing you is to let him go and. in the process, to manage your own fears. You've done a good job raising him; trust that he's capable of learning what he needs to learn in order to go where he wants to go. Trust that your relationship with him can repair enough that he willingly turns to you for guidance and support—*guidance,* not you doing it for him." Bettina took a deep breath and nodded.

"One thing you can do," I counseled her, "is to ask Adam to help you manage your fears. Is there something he could say or do that would be helpful?" Bettina thought awhile and said, "It'd help if we could talk about how we're going to live together between now and then. I'd especially like to talk about curfew."

It turned out that a few weeks before, Adam had unilaterally rebelled and stayed out all night. Bettina had suffered through a very long night. She'd called his friends (an excruciating embarrassment to Adam when he heard about it the next day) and gotten no information about his whereabouts. She'd called his cell phone and gotten voice mail. She was frantic, all alone imagining the worst scenarios.

"I'm not asking for a curfew anymore. I know we're past that point. But I need to know where you are, Adam, and when to expect you."

I said to Adam, "This, too, is about your mom's terror that she might lose you. And that comes out of love and the habit of eighteen years of responsibility for you."

"Yeah," he said with heat. "But why doesn't she trust me! I'm responsible, give me a break!"

"It's new for you to be out in the world and for your mom to have no way to know what's going on. It'll take some time for her to believe you're all right. It's not about your responsibility or competency. It's about her anxiety, which is natural and understandable.

"I get that you felt hopeless about negotiating change with her. But I imagine you didn't help the situation by leaving her to worry for a night. You have the choice to do what you want. You also have the choice to help your mom take care of her feelings in the process so she doesn't fight you. Will you do that?"

Put that way, it was hard for Adam to decline. I'd turned the tables: rather than the discussion assuming her right to control his comings and goings, we were now talking about his power to help and ally with her. "Yeah, I guess so. What would help, Mom?"

"If you'd let me know your plans in advance, and if you'd call and tell me when they change. Actually, if I really got what I wanted, I'd be able to reach you; you'd keep your cell phone on."

"Yeah, OK, no problem. I'd just forgotten to charge the phone. I'll remember." They went on to negotiate details: by what time he'd let her know whether he'd be home for dinner, by what time he'd tell her when he'd be home at night or whether he'd be staying with friends.

The mood was lightening in the room. Adam was sitting up taller.

But I could still feel Bettina's tension. "What else?" I asked her.

"Well, the drugs," she said. "I'm worried that you're stoned all the time, maybe that you're using harder stuff." Drooping dramatically, Adam's head swayed back and forth. It was a gesture at once despairing and angry. He said nothing.

"As long as you're smoking," Bettina went on after a time, color rising on her cheeks, "I'm not giving you an allowance." She was pulling out one of the few forms of material power she had left. He could get himself where he wanted to go in the city without her help, stay out all night, tell her his whereabouts or not. He could go to school or not go to school at will. But at eighteen he faced few resources for obtaining money.

Money is an obvious area of conflict between kids and parents. Early in life, children recognize the value of money in two realms: it is the coin of consumerism, an enticing activity encouraged by huge mega-industries marketing to youngsters; and it is the coin of mastery and control interpersonally. Money is socially denied to children. Their only means of obtaining it for most of the years of childhood is by the arbitrary choice of adults. You get such and such an allowance, at my will. If you don't do your chores, you get no money. So kids begin badgering, negotiating, stealing--using all the powers at their command to gain access to money. In the process they are learning profound lessons about how the world works. In particular, they are experimenting with means to get what they want in life through coercion and manipulation.

Adam's head slowly rose. "I don't want money from you," he declared through clenched teeth. "I won't take an allowance even if you give it. I'll find a job, I'll earn my own way. And meantime, I can do without money."

Adam's strategy was an effective one: to claim the power of withdrawal. In a disadvantaged position, we have one ultimate source of defense: not to want whatever resource lies within others' control. At this point, I intervened, describing the transaction they'd just had in terms of power and escalation. I suggested that Bettina's greater money-earning power constituted a trap. She could use it in a variety of ways, to power play him into doing what she wanted by threatening to withhold money, or by promising rewards for "good" behavior.

But if she did either of those things, she was negating the potential they had of constituting a more egalitarian relationship. Not only did I hold the opinion that parents and adult kids in general had a better time with each other the more they could approximate equality and act cooperatively, but I was also certain that Adam would stop at nothing less than the autonomy and respect such equality offered him. If Bettina power played him with money, he'd escalate the fight in ways she couldn't counter. In other words, in a contest of wills, she'd lose.

Eyes hidden behind his veil of curls, Adam listened attentively. He now said quietly, "I'm smoking dope with friends. But I'm not smoking all the time, not daily, and, because you asked for this, not at home." Both Bettina and I heard the offer of détente in Adam's statement, and also the credibility of his claim. He was not denying that he smoked, but giving Bettina enough detail to be believable.

"I want to believe you," she said. "I guess it'll take a little time for me to believe you all the way."

"And I don't use anything else," Adam continued, responding to her by not responding. "I tried cocaine once and I didn't like it. Some beer sometimes. I don't like drinking much at all. But I don't see what harm pot does, and it helps me with my music."

In a separate chapter, I'll address the problem of distinguishing substance use from substance abuse. The problem for parents is sorting out when to be worried. But Adam and Bettina were performing the critical act: talking about it.

negotiating the transition

Let's extract some principles demonstrated by Bettina and Adam's conversation. Beginning with the most external observations, both Bettina and Adam are white. While they are not affluent—Bettina is a single mom with little family support, none from Adam's father who lives outside the U.S.; she is an artist trying to paint while earning money working in an art supply store—nonetheless their task of confronting issues of school drop-out, drugs, and youth employment is quite different from a comparable situation with African-American or Latino youths. Not only are opportunities for meaningful work far more limited for many young people of color, but dangers on the streets are dramatically more intense. Then too the social judgment about drug use among kids of color tend to be far more harsh than for white youths. Adam is a musician; it is easier to frame his marijuana use as a cultural aspect of the popular music world and to regard it benignly. If he were black, people might well be more alarmed by it, less convinced he was not on the slippery slope to more serious drug use or even dealing, and so on. These racial and ethnic stereotypes rebound on kids, who internalize them as self-image and either suffer erosion of self confidence or play to the theme, "doing drug addict" to the hilt.

Gender matters as well; imagine the scenario if Adam were Alice. Fears about her safety, about sexuality, about deviance from her parental generation's standards of femininity, might well all enter the picture. For young women of color, the stereotypes and restrictions multiply, creating a whole other category of dynamics with which both parents and kids must contend.

How much real danger out in the world a young person faces shapes negotiations at home of power and responsibilities, the hallmark of parenting newly-adult children. Handing over the reins to a grown child when members of his demographic group are frequently gunned down in the streets is a harder task than when you have some reasonable assurance that your child will live out the decade. The transition from a parental relationship of responsibility to one of friendship is aided by freedom from such fears. Nonetheless, what a parent can do is limited, although taking constructive action includes community and political work to combat the conditions breeding violence in our cities, and, on an interpersonal level. Giving good advice to kids can help, although grown kids are far more likely to heed that wisdom if they also experience respect for their independence. The potential for your words to matter is substantial. In any community or culture, once a parent always a parent. But your parent identity effectively matters more if you and your offspring can maintain an emotionally honest relationship that is also flexible, suited to the moment, and mutually respectful.

One crucial part of nurturing that spark of connection between you is remembering to give praise. However feisty and independent your teen may appear, s/he still needs your recognition of her or his strengths and achievements. It's easy to get so distracted by the struggle that you forget to acknowledge the human being. Watch for the things you can genuinely praise, and speak your appreciation often and specifically.

breaking through the other side

Adam and Bettina managed to reconnect, albeit a bit uneasily. They constructed a truce sustained by a hope that the peace would, over time, become rich and rewarding.

Sometimes the ground for reconnecting involves some experience that kids share with parents. Exploring identity is one of those realms, offering opportunities for cross-generational communication and, with it, a heart connection.

Deshon comes from an African-American family that has always demonstrated pride in their racial heritage. On a cultural level, the walls of their home are graced with art from Africa; they celebrate Kwanzaa with a wide circle of friends and family, while also attending a largely-black church; and they have visited Africa and talked frequently about their family's progression from enslavement to middle-class professional status. While the family lives in a black-majority neighborhood, both Deshon's parents work in mainstream institutions, one in the healthcare industry, the other educational. On an experiential level, Deshon and his younger sister have witnessed their parents' success in engaging a multicultural world while maintaining their sense of cultural particularity.

Sandra comes from a highly assimilated Latino family. When they married, her parents moved away from the Spanish enclave where they were raised. They struggled through higher education and achieved middle-class incomes. Their three children were given what they thought of as "Anglo" names, because the parents wanted to protect them from the derision they themselves had experienced from peers as they were growing up.

As a teenager, Sandra felt a hard-to-describe sense of separation from the largely white peer group in which she found herself. She spoke little Spanish (mostly just that which allowed her to decipher her parents' in-Spanish private communication about her). Everyone she dated throughout high school was white, but few of her relationships lasted very long.

LuAnn is third generation Chinese American. For years she watched her mother quarrel with her grandmother, mostly in a language LuAnn couldn't understand. Knowing that her mom had served as interpreter and business agent for her immigrant parents, LuAnn had sympathy for her lack of patience. But she also loved her gentle and attentive grandmother and silently allied with her against their common "enemy."

When LuAnn was a junior in high school, her mother arranged a trip to China for all three generations of the family. They visited the small town that her grandparents came from, saw the homes in which they'd grown up, and heard stories about life for them when they were LuAnn's age. The moment they stepped off the plane, LuAnn felt a profound sense of relief: she actually looked like the majority of people around her. For the first time in her life, she could shed the subtle intrusion of being seen by the world in a way she didn't experience herself: exotic, different, inferior, smart—whatever the assumptions of others might be. But at the same time, LuAnn regretted having resisted learning Cantonese, her grandparents' mother-tongue; she found herself confronting an opposite set of assumptions, as people spoke to her in shops and on the streets believing they shared a common language.

Each of these young people began early in adolescence to struggle with questions of who they were in the greater social world. Deshon felt pride and contentment with his sense of himself as a black American, until he moved from a small, consciously multicultural elementary school into a large public high school that included kids from a wide range of class backgrounds. Black kids tended to group together in social spaces: the cafeteria, a cluster of benches behind the building, a particular section of the boys' locker room. Deshon felt an obligation to join with them, but he felt more familiarity with the racially mixed students who showed up in the math club or who submitted serious entries to the science fair. At the "black table" in the lunchroom, these activities were treated with derision. Deshon looked away in confusion and embarrassment, tinged with more than a little resentment, when his peers labeled the things at which he excelled as "white." At the same time, some of the members of the math club, both students of Asian heritage and whites, seemed to regard him as a rare transplant, somebody to treat with distant respect that hinted of an expectancy of transience. Deshon vowed to himself to be the winner in all categories of math and science when awards were handed out at graduation time, but he also kept his ambitions strictly to himself when hanging out with most of his African-American peers.

Fortunately, there were exceptions. As Deshon's affections waned toward the white and Asian kids with whom he'd been friendly in elementary school, he bonded with two other high-achieving students who were black. They formed a small pocket of comfort and, as the years of high school went on, together they found themselves ever more isolated, more alienated from other streams in the school. Lacking a language to describe the contradictions they were experiencing, none of the three ever talked about it.

Sandra began with the same demographic discoveries as Deshon. But her experience took a very different course. High school was her first encounter with large numbers of Latino kids from very different backgrounds. They came from a wide variety of countries and cultures. Some were bilingual, others not. For some, Spanish was their mother tongue, with English being acquired sometime later when their families immigrated to the U.S. Her friend Sophia's father worked in a warehouse and her mother was a housekeeper in a big downtown hotel. Dominica's mother, on the other hand, was the principal of a large public elementary school and her father was a physician.

For the first time, Sandra experimented with defining herself as Latina. She took up studying Spanish with diligence. She quizzed her parents about their backgrounds, asking them when their ancestors had come to the U.S., how they felt about the fact that her mother's people had been forced by war in the nineteenth century to leave their homeland in what is now New Mexico and move across the modern border into Mexico, only to be legally defined as "immigrants" when, three generations later, they returned to the area from which they'd originally migrated.

Where Deshon found himself contending with layers and complexities of a racial identity he'd thought simple and secure, Sandra joyfully embraced a new identity, adding layers of comfort at the same time she understood in greater depth the subtler impacts of racism on her parents and her own sense of self. Deshon fell silent on the subject, while Sandra discovered her ethnic voice for the first time.

For both teenagers, what they learned about themselves in our very conflictual social world created a distance from their parents. They questioned choices their parents had made about how to negotiate these turbulent waters; Sandra particularly grew angry at her upwardly mobile parents' decision to isolate from their extended families and communities of birth.

LuAnn, meanwhile, had an experience that brought her closer to her mother. She realized that they were on a similar track, her mother seeking to reclaim an identity that had been compromised by her childhood-established role in the family, while LuAnn began to see herself in the context of her origins, even while she explored her individuality.

All three teenagers' parents contended with their own feelings about these changes. Each family had thought to protect their youngsters from destructive racial and ethnic dynamics in society. While Deshon's family had managed to connect to a larger middle class black community, a warmly welcoming group of neighbors and fellow church-goers, they now sensed their son's censure for having protected him from very complicated, interlocking themes of class, culture, gender, and race. Sandra was overtly angry at her parents for isolating the family from their culture of origin and for suppressing (as she saw it) their history of oppression and survival. But at the same time she wished to protect them from her anger, understanding with fresh vividness what they had suffered as the children of immigrants while climbing a splintery ladder of status and class. LuAnn discovered greater respect for her mother as the older woman established a greater sense of her own cultural integrity.

White families far less often are aware of confronting such dimensions of generational development. For both parents and children, membership in the mainstream seems to afford a more seamless sense of self, one that is more consistent with the way one is seen by others and with the dominant culture. Cathy Toshiro, a sociologist who focuses on matters of identity among mixed race persons, delineates five distinct dimensions of racial identity: cultural identity (core values and ways of being in the world), ascribed identity (the way a person is seen by others), identification to others (how one labels oneself in communication with the outside world), self-identification (how one thinks of oneself), and situational identity (how one feels identified in particular circumstances). Deshon, LuAnn, and Sandra likely felt differently about themselves at home versus at school, more or less black or Chinese or Latina depending on the company they were keeping. Their cultural identities and self identities were shifting month by month as they explored their social personhood. Yet the identities ascribed to them by those closest to them—by other family members, old friends, and so on—as well as by those most distant--passers-by in the street, police officers, or people regarding them with a sexualized eye—remained constant.

Teenagers of all races who explore queer sexual orientations have other versions of these tensions and shifts. High school years are a time when most youths experiment with sex and sexuality. Whether heterosexual, homosexual, or transgendered, adolescents encounter the intersection of hormonal development, social ascription of categories—what are you? Gay? Lesbian? Bi?, etc.—and the beginnings of autonomy in intimate relationships outside the family. For gay teens, though, the waters may be stormy and dangerous. Despite the growing chic of queer culture in the media, gay young people continue to face name-calling, sexual predation, and a thousand other forms in which their compromised status is communicated. Meanwhile, whether out to parents or not, they may be feeling, or fearing, the severity of this particular identity breach at home. For much of America, homosexuality is still a feared and morally censured category of human experience. Many parents "rise to the occasion" and place their love for their kids above whatever moral rules they've been taught. One father I know, a fifth generation member of a fundamentalist Christian church in a small town, was surprised to discover his fury at his community when his daughter announced her lesbianism and the congregation quietly shunned not only her, but himself, his wife, and their other two children as well. His wife decamped to another church, but he insisted on showing up every Sunday and, in as public a way as possible, making known some new piece of information dispelling myths about gay people.

But other family stories are not as bracing. I've heard of parents who beseeched their children to keep their orientation secret from relatives and friends. Others have wrestled with their kids to "change their minds." I've worked in therapy with both men and women whose families disowned them, in one case casting their daughter out so thoroughly that they performed rituals of exorcism to purify their home.

For parents in these families, the challenge is not only to their capacity for acceptance of differences but also, often, to their own unexamined relationship to sexuality. That is not to say that parents may find that they are unconsciously gay; that is a psychological myth that generates misunderstanding. But to internalize homophobia may also rule out of acceptability ranges of sensuality, of passion, and joyfulness that contradict rules that dictate obligation and responsibility. Our society tends to pit these categories against each other. Hedonism is feared and repressed, the idea being that if left to our own unbridled desires we would run amok and never get anything done. In our task-oriented culture, that is distinctly not all right. The repression of sex, therefore, carries with it an alienation from the strata of human experience that is suggested by homosexuality. If sex is purely about pleasure, passion, and intimacy, then what becomes of bedrock institutions, of marriage and the family and concentrated productivity, in unrewarding jobs tolerated for the sake of responsibility to those families?

By extension, a core prejudice against gay people is that the pursuit of sexual pleasure dictates their life choices. It is a small step to fears of gay pedophilia or "recruitment" of young people to gay lifestyles. One would hope that the gay baby boom well underway as I write, not to mention the ardent campaigning to legalize same-sex marriage, might prove the point that a similar range of life choices applies across the spectrum of sexual orientation: as many gay people as straight want to marry and raise children; as many (actually, statistically more) straight men are sexual offenders as gay men. Similar dynamics may operate, too, when kids veer in occupational directions that run counter to parents' values or when they enter into interracial or cross-class or mixed religion relationships. As a parent of a teen, your task is to sort through your own forsaken ambitions, loves, and creativity to acknowledge and, perhaps, mourn the paths not taken in your own life, and then to manage your reactions to your kids' choices with care and love and discipline.

From the moment you first put that baby to nipple or bottle, to now when you watch your fledglings fly awkwardly off in many directions at once, returning nonetheless with mouths wide open to receive your sustenance, your task has developed and changed, and always remained the same: take care of yourself so you can respond with openness and honesty. Perhaps it is not surprising that the stories I've recounted in this chapter are such challenging ones; difficulty is the quality popularly associated with parenting teenagers. Yet the other side of that coin is the mourning I hear from parents as they anticipated the passage of kids from home to world. "My lovely little boy," Jerome lamented. "To me, he's still that cuddly child carrying his favorite book to me at bedtime. I can't stand the idea that he'll soon be all grown up and gone away!"

Of course, Jerome can and will stand it, no doubt with all the pride and delight he's experienced right along. How often parents nearing the end of this stage revel in a new-found ability to stand back and see their children as formed adults in the world, people whom they still regard with enormous love and hope.

7

s/he's leaving home, bye bye:
parenting young adults

Developmental challenges:
1) Reclaiming personhood

So they've left home, going off to college or the military, or taking the harder path of knocking around the world trying to find a calling or simply a job. You've negotiated the best of times, the worst of times. Your nest is empty (or at least one of the chicks has fledged).

Congratulate yourself. You've succeeded in maintaining life until some version of adulthood has been achieved by your offspring, some version of liberation for yourself (actually, for you both).

In the event, though, you don't know whether to feel depressed or relieved. Thank heaven you've made it to this point. But what are you supposed to do with all that energy, physical and emotional, now?

And then the phone rings.

"I'm having a little problem here."

Or, not quite so bad, "Send money."

Or, a little better still, "I need some advice." (Feel proud s/he still sees you as having something worthwhile to give that's not hard cash.)

Or, best of all, "Guess what great and wondrous thing just happened that I want to share with you!"

Eighteen is here... and parenting isn't done. What now? Parenting books tend to stop at high school graduation, but I very often hear from people struggling with questions about how to *relate* to their grown children.

If all the stages you've traversed up until now were guided by principles of power sharing, this one carries on the tradition, but with greater subtlety and fewer guidelines. How do you continue to support and guide your now-young-adult without taking on the thankless—and hopeless—tasks of dictate and control? Is sending money disempowering Rescue or parental responsibility? What if you and your co-parent disagree?

And what in the world do you do if they show up on your doorstep wanting to move back home?

Studies show that the most highly stressful position a person can occupy is one with a lot of responsibility and very little power. Middle managers have the highest rates of heart attack. I'd wonder if parents of eighteen-year-old fledglings might not have the next highest rates, especially as the youth perches unsteadily on the edge of the nest, just about to take off but not yet gone.

catalyst for conflict: return of the simmons

We last encountered the Simmons in Chapter 3, when Jimmy was five and Jenny three. Everyone survived and now it is Thanksgiving, the first holiday home from college for Jimmy. Grandma Sally has flown in for the holiday and Julia's parents have arrived as well, carrying pies and potions. Aside from mild and familiar skirmishes in the kitchen between Julia and her mom, everyone is reasonably mellow and seated in their places before a laden table.

Julia wipes a sweaty lock from her forehead and says, "Let's join hands and give thanks for all of our blessings this year." Taking her father's hand on her left, she bows her head and reaches for Jimmy's hand with her right.

"I don't believe in *blessings*," Jimmy says with a sneer. He puts his hand in hers but looks defiantly around the table and declares, "We make our own blessings!"

Julia jerks her hand away, Joe laughs robustly, and Thanksgiving, new style, has begun.

There are two themes I hear repeatedly at this stage of parenting: the first is an offspring's shift from angry combatant to haughty critic, and the second is a new wave of warfare engendered between co-parents.

Think in terms of power and the Rescue Triangle. If as a teenager Jimmy was fighting for all he was worth to escape his status as dependent, and if he did that by rebelling in all ways available to him, now he has achieved a full measure of physical independence. He lives apart from his family and reappears in their midst as visitor. He brings with him a life in which he has chosen his bedtime, chosen his meals, chosen his companions, chosen whether or not to do his homework, even whether or not to show up for classes.

At the same time, need for his parents still nips inchoately at his heels. They may contribute substantially to his financial existence. Even more, despite his best effort, which takes the form of disdain for their opinions, he wants them to think well of him. A stubborn particle of his psyche is still the two-year-old tugging at his mother's clothing and saying, "Watch me go down the slide! Look what I can do!" Not having found a way to feel about that need, to dignify it as one of many threads in the love that binds him with (not to) his mother, he still experiences himself as needy, as a Victim to his mother's Rescue. As he vainly tries to cram the two-year-old Jimmy into a sound-proofed box, he finds emanating from himself instead a voice laden with Persecution and still speaking of dependence.

Julia, meanwhile, regards her son with all the pride he could wish, but she is still preoccupied with her role as mom, expressed this day in terms of turkey and kitchen diplomacy vis-à-vis her own mother. To join hands around the abundance she has wrought is, for her, to recharge her waning batteries. Instead, depletion is compounded. From Rescue, she plunges to Victim and immediately, as is her habit, responds with angry Persecution.

Joe in turn watches the family drama unfold with a familiar sense of helplessness and responsibility, his historic role uneasily combining Victim with Rescue, all the more intensified by the scrutiny of his mother and Julia's parents. Doesn't he sit at the head of this prototypic family table? And isn't that supposed to mean something about how he's supposed to intervene? Alas, at the moment it doesn't suggest anything much at all. He laughs to lighten the tension, the only act he can think of, and not exactly a voluntary act at that. Underneath, he laughs as well to ally himself with Jimmy, a wee Persecution of Julia in return for what he, too, has long experienced as the imposition of what he secretly considers her quasi-religious, touch-feely values.

Jenny, too, finds herself in a new version of her old role. These months since Jimmy left for college, she has felt relief from the constant bickering and tensions between brother and mother, mother and father. Having laid low and looked away for years, focusing all that time on self-defense, and having attained her own full adolescence, she has just begun to stretch a bit, to experience herself moving from sideline to center, even beginning to dip a toe into self-assertion. She does not laugh at Jimmy's declaration. She folds her arms crossly and looks away with evident revulsion and anger. For years she has tried to absent herself from the family dynamic, but now she allows herself far more expression. As her mother turns on her father in protest, she throws her napkin down and stomps away from the table.

For that is how Julia does respond. Her wrath turns not on Jimmy, her darling, but on Joe. Ally and enemy are common positions that parents adopt in relationship to children, and those sides become all the more polarized at this stage. For one thing, the behaviors associated with them are condensed into the span of occasional visits. Earlier, the jostling of conflict around a child identified as The Problem was a daily event, an assumed part of family life that was so constant it became invisible. Now, the same dynamic is played out, almost literally, as theatre around the holidays: events with a clear time definition, a beginning and an end, a plot and a purpose. And there is an audience: the presence of other family members both encourages the drama and shames the actors, for it adds layers of shadow and memories of intergenerational histories that are the backdrop for Joe and Julia's responses, shaping their own behaviors through dynamics of incorporation and resistance; the very same dynamics Jimmy and Jenny now experience.

Like Jenny, the parents have also enjoyed a brief reprieve from all this conflict. Hope was nurtured by a series of sweet phone calls from Jimmy at the beginning of the semester. "Mom," he said excitedly on the first call, "Guess what I'm learning about in my philosophy class!" And he went on to describe "this neat prof," along with anecdotes from the first lecture.

"Dad," he said when Joe got on the phone, "what do you think I should do about email? I can get a university account, but I kind of want to keep my AOL screen name, too. Can we pay for both?"

In the first months away, Jimmy called with questions and exuberance many times. Joe and Julia were touched and encouraged by the initiative he took to be in contact. They felt affirmed by his delight in sharing joys with them and his continued need for their counsel.

So Thanksgiving was a rude awakening and a moment for renegotiating their parenting roles. Taken by surprise, the Simmons momentarily forgot what they had learned over the years about sharing power; they tumbled, straight down the rabbit hole, into their old roles.

But only briefly. With all the grandparents safely on their way back to their respective homes, feelings in the Simmons household began to settle out. Everyone retired to a comfort zone for awhile: Julia tidied the kitchen, Jenny listened to music in her room, Joe and Jimmy watched the TV news.

It was Jenny who started the talk-ball rolling. Sliding onto the couch beside her dad, she waited for a commercial and then addressed her brother.

"What's up with you, Jimmy? Why'd you do that at the table?"

Jimmy stared at the TV screen for a long beat. "Yeah, why did I?" he reflected. "You know, I think we need to talk. Dad, are you game? Let's pry Mom out of the kitchen."

Change in the order of things, number one: talk was initiated by the children, not the parents.

(It was just a little beyond this time in my own parenting history, by the way, that my partner challenged the terminology I used. "It doesn't seem right to call ourselves 'parents' anymore, and they certainly aren't children. How about we're the 'rents' and they're the 'rens'?" The language never took hold, but the notion did.)

Jimmy apologized for "being a brat" right away, and Julia expressed her surprise and hurt at what he'd said. Julia also formally addressed Joe's laugh ("I felt angry and alone," she said), and Joe told her how he'd felt when she'd turned on him (embarrassed, confused, hurt). Jenny told Jimmy and Julia both how sad and angry and tired she was of their getting into conflict with each other.

The air cleared, they began to untangle the why of it, a step toward figuring out what change was in the making.

"You know," Jimmy began, "I think it was really hard for me to come home and be subject to your ways of doing things. It's not like I hated it so much before I left for school, but now that I've been on my own, it just feels so backward to come home and have no say. I'm not sure I can do it."

"But this is still *my* home, mine and your dad's, and for the time being Jenny's, too. Why should we all march to *your* tune?" Julia replied.

Jenny glanced at her brother and said, "Well, actually mom, I've never really liked that blessings business at Thanksgiving, either. We don't do anything like that all year long; it just feels phony to do it when your parents are around, just because it's what they did when you were a kid."

Julia rejoined, "It's not *just* because they did." She held up her hand for silence as both offspring began to speak. "Let me think about that for a minute. I guess maybe you're right; I am trying to please them. Or maybe to hide from them how different I am. I guess I'm not really so committed to reciting blessings in that way."

Jimmy and Jenny glanced at each other quickly. Jimmy said, "Thanks, Mom. I really appreciate your coming clean about that. I'm not expecting everything to be my way when I come home. But I guess I'm trying not to do what you were just doing, to pretend to you to be some way I'm not."

"OK, Jimmy. I'm sorry I went along with my assumptions about how we'd be. I get that we need to consult with you more. And you, too, Jenny.

"Let's each think about how, ideally, we'd like to celebrate Christmas and New Year's. I'll figure out what really matters to me, and you all do the same. Then let's talk through some new rituals. Will you each do that?" She looked at Joe in a meaningful way.

Joe smiled and nodded vigorously. His relief was evident, but so was his silence. "You don't have to ask me what I'm thinking," he said quickly. "I know, I know. I'm thinking about it." They all waited.

"OK, here it is," he said at length. "I'm not as quick as the rest of you about knowing what I feel, but I actually felt pretty proud of Jimmy when he spoke up and angry at you, Julia, when you jumped all over him.

"But I'm not feeling much of that right now. I'm really relieved we've gotten this far. Negotiating stuff is not that hard for us; we've done it a long time, we've just got to remember to do it.

"It makes total sense, Jimmy, that even after a couple of months of living on your own you'd feel different about being back home. Onward, toward Christmas!"

A conversation like this one is not far fetched when you've been learning since the birth of your child to read, name, and negotiate power. What I've written here closely follows similar conversations I've heard often in my office. Jimmy and Jenny are skilled at knowing what they feel; they have become able partners in the process. Julia and Joe have practiced (possibly under even harder conditions) by applying these same skills to their own relationship.

Three principles for parenting in this stage of life emerge from the Simmons' story:

- Embrace the new order: Kids lead, parents guide, everyone negotiates.
- Enjoy the new space for your own emotional honesty and your feelings and needs, even as you explore the new fulcrum at which power balances.
- Open yourself to new ideas and relationships brought home by your fledglings. Expect improvements rather than rejections.

Simple principles can be hard to apply. Let's go to stories of older kids and play them out in more detail.

support or rescue? or a little of each...

Adopted as an infant from Davinda's homeland of India, Sencia was a wonder kid. Loving and compliant, she was a straight A student all through elementary and high school. Her counselors assured her that she could gain admission to almost any college, and she chose a super-high-status ivy league one. Her fathers, both successful professionals, Stanlee in law and Davinda in engineering, were happy with her choice and glad to fund her. As the first generation to achieve professional stature in their respective families, they looked forward to Sencia's surpassing even their achievements. She chose a pre-med track and dived into labs and higher math and another string of As.

Sencia's dads had raised her with discipline and clarity. They believed in "setting limits," which to them meant imposing "time-outs" as corrections for behavior they adjudged deficient. Fortunately for them, Sencia had usually been compliant. She was, as they delighted in describing her to friends and family, a "natural pleaser," almost uncanny in her ability to detect what they wanted from her and then to do it. Even as a teenager, she'd been easy, although there was a year when she barely spoke. Stan and Davinda worried she might be depressed, but her grades continued to be good and they got only positive reports about her from school and other parents. So they packed her off to college with full assurance that she'd come back in a few years as a talented physician.

In her sophomore year, Sencia came home for winter break and Davinda immediately sensed something was different. Her hair was shorn unevenly, her earrings didn't match, her eyes were thickly lined in magenta. It seemed to Davinda she was distant or distracted or troubled. He spoke with Stan about it, but Stan pooh-poohed him. "Why are you looking for problems where none exist?" he asked. "She's fine, it's the style these days. She's just maybe a little tired."

But Sencia was more than tired. She was burned out on the success track. One night at dinner, she grew quiet and at length announced, "I have something to tell you. I'm not going back to school. I don't want to be a doctor. I want to paint."

"You can't!" Davinda exclaimed.

"Let's be calm and think about this," intervened Stanlee.

More shouting than thinking proceeded over the rest of the holiday. Positions solidified. Davinda grieved and raged and raised provocative questions: "And just how do you plan to support yourself?" Stanlee reasoned and counseled and supported: "Well, it's a lovely thing you've discovered art, and I'm sure you're really, really talented. I still have that great leopard painting you did in first grade."

At night, behind the closed door of their bedroom, they fought. "How can you support her in this nonsense!?" Davinda fumed.

"I'm sure it's a phase," Stan countered. "We should stand by her while she finds herself."

"Finds herself, my ass!" Davinda screamed. "She's never been lost before. I'll bet there's some boy in this story!"

The more Stanlee went for calm, the more upset Davinda grew.

Three years later, Stan and Davinda had parted ways. Sencia had made good on her decision to leave college; she now lived with a boy-friend in an apartment they shared with three other people. She took a community college art class from time to time, trying out different genre: figurative one month, abstract the next. Now she was "into" per-formance art, something neither of her fathers understood.

Stanlee was still supportive, though, even if privately he shook his head more and more often in confusion and concern. He paid Sencia's rent and sent her money whenever she asked, which was often. Now she was asking him to fund a studio, an expensive proposition made more so because she claimed she needed a whole list of costly com-puter equipment in order to take her creativity to the next level. At last, Stanlee didn't immediately consent; instead, he said he needed to consult with Davinda.

Davinda meanwhile had developed a pattern of giving Sencia mon-ey even while he endlessly berated her and placed hollow conditions on the hand-out: "Be sure you use this for....." whatever he thought she should be doing next. Sencia um-hmm-ed him dutifully, took the dough and did what she pleased. But she was also growing increasingly surly. For the first time in any of their experience, she jabbed at Davin-da, teasing him about his accent, making fortuitous jokes about dumb engineers. Davinda was hurt, but swallowed his pride in his attempt to maintain the role of limit-setter he believed was his responsibility. He and Stanlee rarely talked about how to handle things with Sencia, but privately each criticized the other.

The humongous bill for computer equipment tipped the balance. Stanlee phoned Davinda and, after a little posturing, they both con-fessed they hadn't a clue what to do. They decided it was time for help, so they proposed to Sencia that they go together to mediation. Seeing the process as a means to the end of getting the stuff she wanted, Sencia agreed.

How much responsibility do parents bear for providing financial support to their young adult children as they get started in life? Davinda drew on the language of addiction treatment to call Stanlee's behavior "enabling." Substance abuse is one of the few metaphors in current cultural usage seeking to describe human dynamics. But it sheds at least as much dust as light on the subject. The implication that Sencia was "addicted"--to what? To her fathers' money? To art? To sloth?—is value-laden and inaccurate, not to mention harmfully judgmental. The kernel of truth in that formulation is that her parents' choices might promote a troubling dependency. Sometimes necessity is in fact the mother of invention. To be buffered from the need someday to earn a living was, for Sencia, to be Rescued in a way that could become debilitating.

That was clearly one of Davinda's fears, that she would never achieve financial independence if they continued to support her, because she'd never be forced to learn the hard lessons that lead to that end. Stanlee, on the other hand, believed she was learning plenty at the moment. "She's only twenty-two, and she's trying to do something really hard: be an artist."

Like so many other questions about child-rearing, this one has no simple answer. In mediation, I asked Sencia to talk fully about her life, her vision, and her hopes. She confessed that she was less focused on making art than she had imagined when she'd first declared herself an artist. "There are times when I'm making a piece and I just lose myself. I love those moments. But they don't come often, and at other times, quite honestly, I'm bored.

"I think I just need time to explore," she said thoughtfully. "College didn't really give me that, because I was already so socked into a particular track. And maybe because I did so well everyone just assumed I'd be a doctor, and I just couldn't assume it anymore."

I asked her what she had learned about herself so far. "I know I need creativity in my life, but I also know that can take lots and lots of forms. I could even imagine being a creative doctor. I know I need to learn things in my own way, by doing as much as by reading.

"And I also know," she added, "that I'm not happy depending on my parents for money. I want to be on my own eventually. I just don't know how to get there yet."

Next, I asked each parent to talk about his personal experience of class and money. Stanlee told Sencia what it had meant to come from a working class family and to be the first to go to college. Becoming a lawyer was something no one in his blue-collar background had accomplished. He was held in such high regard that sometimes he was uneasy about it. "I had no room to explore, the way you are," he said with some sadness. "I knew from a little kid that I needed to do better than my parents, and I just plodded ahead and did that."

"Not that I regret it," he quickly added. "But I sometimes wonder what I might have discovered if I could have had some time not to know my path." He went on to talk about the unexpected pain of having fulfilled his family's dreams for him. "Sometimes it's hard to talk to them. They don't know how I live, and I can't really relate to how they live anymore. I feel both responsible and guilty for being so well off. I think you know that I help support them, too." That estrangement born of class mobility was compounded by his sexuality. "Bless their hearts, they really work hard to be accepting, but I know it's troubling for them that I'm gay, even after all these years."

Davinda then described what it was for him to have stayed on in the U.S. after earning his graduate degree here. "You've met my folks," he said. "They look and often sound really familiar because they're very westernized and highly educated. But I know they are really unhappy that I'm not there with them, that I didn't do the eldest son thing, bring a bride and grandchildren into their home. Even now, they ask me whether I might not find the right girl--or even better, let them find her for me—and come back.

"Of course," he said plaintively, "that hurts. There's no way I could, not only because I'm gay, but because I've grown so far away from them culturally." He fell silent for a moment.

"The least I could do along the way was to pay my own way," he said at last. "I couldn't possibly rely on them for anything. That would be adding insult to injury."

Davinda's hard line with Sencia made as much sense as Stanlee's soft one. This kind of dialogue was new for the three of them. In its structure as well as it's content, it mapped a new type of equality, each of them showing up as a distinct individual with a moving and credible story.

None of which exactly told them how to proceed, but it did open some space for viewing their individual stories in a greater context. Years ago, my colleague and friend Becky Jenkins came up with a developmental schema for the decades of adulthood:

- The Twenties are for precisely what Sencia was doing: exploration.
- The Thirties are for gaining skills that enable us to do the things we've discovered are right for us.
- The Forties are for locating the doing in society, for establishing credibility and, perhaps, a career.
- The Fifties are for gaining acknowledgement for all we are and have done.
- The Sixties are for learning how to rest and remembering how to play.

(Of course, nowadays there's every possibility that work will go on well beyond the Sixties, and life will go on well past Seventy.)

Not everyone has the latitude to do it this way. Many of us are constrained by economics and community values that pressure us to begin life-long careers right away. Or at least to think we're beginning life-long careers; social scientists actually predict that a young person starting out today will have at least seven different "careers" before retirement so rapidly is the economy changing.

Money is a huge factor limiting the scope of experimentation and voluntary re-tooling of careers. In a just society, I believe, we would provide community support for such a process. Instead, too many peo-

ple are locked into working lives that are alienated, offering little satisfaction beyond a pay check and often subjecting employees to hours of
tedium, if not worse. They are locked in, that is, right up to the moment
when the factory moves abroad or technology overcomes labor and the
worker is dispensed with.

In a world where young people receive adequate social support-
-where education is truly free and jobs are plentiful, for instance, and
where health care is universal and public transportation viable—the
help of parents beyond childhood is largely redundant. Today's America,
however, doesn't offer those resources, and so families need pick up the
slack when they can and in the ways they can. How and how much
are the questions that bring us back to Stanlee, Davinda, and Sencia's
dilemma.

After I had sketched these themes and ideas, urging them toward
a substantial release from expectations and recriminations all around,
the dads asked Sencia to make a plan for the next year (or longer, if
she could). They'd support her exploration with the understanding that
that's what it was, a creative alternative to college. What they needed in
return was a greater sense of her path, how she was doing and where
she needed to go next.

"OK, here's what I think I'd like," Sencia began. "I'd like to have a
year of support, so I can play with different ways of making art. Forget
the computer equipment; I can probably make do with an extension
class I've found. That'll give me access to what I need."

"Great," said Davinda. "But here are a couple of things that would
help me feel supportive of what you're doing: Some career counseling,
for starters. It sounds to me that you're confused about what you want
to do; I'd like you to get some help sorting that out.

"Then, too, whatever you do, I think college degrees matter. Would
you explore degree programs, even if they're in fine arts? I'd be happier
if I knew you'd be getting a bachelor's degree somewhere down the
line. You don't have to start right away. In fact, you might find you don't

want to go that route at all. But I'd like to know you had looked into it and made an informed choice."

Sencia agreed to the latter but not to counseling. "I appreciate the offer, but I'm not ready. I feel I'm making progress doing what I'm doing now. I want to play it out longer."

"What comes to my mind," Stanlee contributed, "is the idea of talking with some artists who do support themselves financially. I'm thinking of my friend Stefania, and also maybe Davinda's cousin Satia. Wouldn't it be helpful to know how they pull that off?"

I asked Sencia whether she'd ever held a paying job; babysitting in high school was about as much earning as she'd done. "What about getting some sort of part-time work, just so you begin to gain confidence in your ability to get a paycheck?" I asked. I went on to say that I thought it was especially unjust that American society did so little to back up artists, unlike some Scandinavian and Asian societies that either bought art or otherwise subsidized creative production. Artists I knew either struggled with scarce teaching jobs or managed to find paid work that didn't interfere with making art and sometimes actually harmonized with it: working with young children in creative ways, making crafts, or doing design jobs.

Sencia hesitated, then admitted she was scared by the notion. "All the more reason to take it on," I argued. "There are skills to learn about landing and handling jobs, especially those you don't really want. You'll need some sources of support and teaching along the way perhaps, maybe counseling, or an on-going conversation with peers confronting the same demands."

"Well, there is a coffee house in my neighborhood where a friend works," Sencia said. "I could try there."

Sencia was fortunate in having access to resources (at least, we hope in the end it turns out to have been good fortune). Many, many families cannot help financially. An extra margin of funds that can be dedicated to launching grown children is a mark of privilege. But less affluent families do many other kinds of things to help—providing housing for older offspring, doing childcare for grandchildren while their parents work, or hosting elaborate weekly family dinners that subsidize the weekly food budget. Many grandparents take on the care of children whose parents are struggling with drug use, incarceration, or poverty. The phenomenon of older guardians of very young children is major and deserves a book to itself, written by someone who's been there.

course corrections

Davinda and Stan needed to overcome earlier assumptions about parental responsibility, as well as opening themselves to new perceptions of who their daughter was. It often happens that parents may only recognize the necessity of easing off parental control when their offspring are old enough to have the option of staying away. Younger children are captive to the social structures we are given. We have no *ghotul* (the youth house I mentioned in the last chapter). For all the pulling and rebelling and withdrawal teenagers may do, their choices are usually still severely limited: either buckle under or hit the road. I've worked with kids who did the later, and quickly changed their minds about the wisdom of homelessness. They may still have fought hard with parents, but they also yielded at an earlier point having tested the extremes.

But once they've moved away, the choices are very different. In most families, the ultimate power children have is to stay away. There are parents, of course, who will write off their young. I've already mentioned some I've known who have done that over issues of homosexuality or, in extreme cases, religious and political differences.

Mostly, though, parents will give in, at least a bit, under the threat of losing contact altogether. As teens still living at home, the child's best strategy is to be unrelentingly obnoxious. But now s/he has the even more powerful option of simply saying, "You won't see me until you shape up."

So how do you start now to recognize the rights of your young adult children without having to undergo a power struggle of such severity? And how do you do it with dignity? You must first work through any mistrust your son or daughter has of your will to negotiate genuinely. Accustomed to the power struggle, kids may go on struggling well beyond the point when parents seek to find another way.

It's helpful first to name the change you wish to make and second, to apologize for mistakes that you feel, in retrospect, you've made. Stating the change is the easier of these two tasks. It can be as simple as saying, "Let's find another way to get along. I miss you and love you and want a really satisfying relationship with you."

Apologizing is an art form. Mostly, we're familiar with coerced apologies, which commonly sound something like, "I'm sorry I was a bad person. (Don't hit me again!)" A genuinely helpful apology must be both genuine and self-forgiving. If you beat yourself up, the person hearing you will have a hard time buying into your statement, no matter how mad s/he may be at you. Search your history for the things you did or thought or believed that you now wish you'd been able to do differently. Punishment, for instance, whether corporal or in the form of deprivations, may well have fueled miseries of rebellion at certain stages throughout the child's life. If you now have awareness of alternatives you didn't know about then, your apology might be something like this: "I wish I had learned more about how to handle things without punishing you when you were younger. I thought I was being a responsible parent, but I can see now that I confused control with responsibility. I'm really sorry if, as I suspect, that mistake created a breach between us. Now I'd like to get on a different track, to see if we can make a better relationship."

Apologies depend on something that is a critical skill for parenting —indeed, for all cooperative relationships: being able to see the context. I started this book articulating a basic premise from which I work, that people are neither bad nor crazy, that we feel the things we feel and do the things we do for good reasons. Problems in relationships feed on the inability of one person to see the context in which another feels and acts. A two-year-old temper tantrum can be seen out of context as an expression of endless will on the part of an uncivilized creature. Or it can be seen in context as a means for a youngster who is just beginning to experience ever-widening sources of power, as well as the limits to that power, to express needs and wants with vigor.

So, too, we tend to view our own behaviors out of context, substituting instead self-recrimination, a form of internalized oppression: *I was too authoritarian back then because I'm a control freak.* Or, *I submitted to the will of my partner against my better judgment because I'm weak and dumb.*

In contrast, a contextualized understanding of mistakes assumes one made choices for reasons which were compelling and understandable at the time. But in the reckoning of those decisions certain errors now become visible that were not visible back then, although they may have been sensed without language even at that time. The key here is to see your own mistakes of the past as lesson plans for the present: What do I need to learn? I can't change the past, but what do I need to change now and for the sake of what future goal?

Having learned to establish this forgiving and constructive relationship with yourself, you're well-placed to do the same with partners, spouses, friends, co-workers, and, especially, with children. Kids sense the difference between judgment and compassionate criticism. They may not respond immediately, for time is sometimes needed to establish new trust. But respond they will eventually. The healing involved in that practice is aided by space as well as time. Living separately is a great help in turning the corner toward a new, less conflict-full relationship.

when the nest stays full

But what about those cases when there is no space between parents and adult kids? An increasingly typical scenario in these strained economic times is the adult child who does not leave home, or, driven by financial problems, returns after a brief time away.

If it was difficult for Jimmy to come home for Thanksgiving after a couple of months away, it can be even more difficult for an adult offspring who's been away and needs to move back in with parents after being on her or his own. Patterns of living together as parent and child become deeply etched in habit, for both generations. Easy expectations lead to conflict: that a parent will do the laundry or a "child" will set the table, that the younger generation is more responsible for accounting to the older for comings and goings than the other way around, that sexuality at home is the right of parents but not of offspring. All the more persuasive (but equally insidious) are old expectations when the child has not left home but goes on living there beyond high school or the age of eighteen.

The keynote here is the word "expectations." Recognize them and reconsider. Start negotiating relationships from scratch, maybe as a ritual of a child's eighteenth birthday.

Renegotiation does not mean, however, that the rights now lie all with the younger member of the family. Everyone's rights continue to be equal, as they (hopefully) have been right along. Parents get to, indeed *need* to, be honest about their own wishes and needs. Three changes happen at this stage: First, children's needs become very different. Adult kids need freedom to come and go and explore life on their own terms. They need spaces in which to explore sexuality (not that that probably hasn't already been happening, in today's world, for some time). They need room for socializing with peers in their own ways.

The second change is in that by-now familiar realm, power. Parents still have marginally more power than their offspring because the home they co-inhabit is still the parents' home. But kids have more power than they had before, because they have greater (although clearly not sufficient) mobility and because they, ideally, have more adult responsibilities, the third realm in which change is taking place.

Wherever possible, this is a time for children to contribute financially, as well as to take on more adult responsibility for the care and upkeep of the environment that they're sharing with their parents. To some degree, they are now living with parents by choice (even though their choices may be seriously constrained by finances.) Before, power and responsibility was apportioned in the context of involuntary relationships: parents were responsible to house, feed, and support their youngsters because society does not offer other arrangements (not, at least, in any humanely satisfactory form). Now parental responsibility does not necessarily include those acts. People are living together by agreement, not by necessity.

There are nuances of power and responsibility involved in these adult-to-adult/parent-and-child relationships. Nobody has a blueprint, but there is a process—the same one I've been suggesting all along. Begin by talking honestly, starting with each person's vision of how he or she would like living together to work now. Identify the differences in vision and negotiate solutions, rather than letting those differences show up as wearying, daily conflicts. If you get stuck, talk to others in your community, for there are likely to be other people forging pathways through the same new territory.

One word to the wise: while you may need to craft living-together arrangements as if you are new roommates, keep in mind that you are not. To your strapping, bearded son or your competent, all-grown up daughter, you are still mom or dad. Your power to impose your judgments may be diminished but it is not gone. If your agreement is not to Rescue, and not to power play as strategies for getting your way, then remember that disapproval is a greater act of coercion from parent to child than the other way around.

getting more equal all the time

Emotional ties do go two ways. When my sons, now in their thirties, fly, I am always aware of it, always just a little tense. The emotional umbilical cord that in an earlier time made their forays into the physical world beyond my reach truly fearful (however well I managed and masked my fear!) now exists as a shadow. On the other side, my feelings about their life choices hold a lot less weight for them than they once did. But they do still matter. I know that my disapproval looms larger than the man-in-the-street's. I also know that my compliments, my appreciation of their accomplishments and talents, and manifold manifestations of self also affect them significantly. What my opinions do *not* do, however, is mold them anymore. My reactions are just that: the reactions of a loved and important character in their lives, but not a determinant of what they do or do not do.

Of course, I also relish *their* approval, and I'm unhappy when they judge my actions critically. They have power to affect my mood, too. But the impact is not the same. Knowing that added shade of power that my emotional reactions have, I am a shade more disciplined than I might be with my partner or my friend, to voice my feelings without judgment. I try to be honest because that's always been our deal. But I think through charged feelings and sort out the part that is about me, about my sense of self, from the part that is about them. And I try to infuse what I do say with the genuine love and admiration I feel for them, in a way that supports and does not undermine their route through life, even when (very occasionally these days) I raise questions about their choices.

Aside from that asymmetry, just about everything else is now equal between us. A delicious part of that transformation is the emotional sup-port I get from them. The other day, I finished a string of sessions with clients who had suffered particularly painful experiences; one had just been the victim of crime, another received a frightening diagnosis, and a third had decided to divorce. At the end of the day, I knew I needed help handling the human pain I'd helped others handle all day. I invited myself in for a cup of tea with Josh and his partner, Kendra. Their love and respect, their wisdom and humor, were just what I needed. Often, my partner and I have long, delicious conversations with Tuhin and his partner about life and relationships and politics and art. They are among our most prized friends.

Still, there are times when watching grown kids struggle to get a foothold in life is challenging. Each time the adult child faces a difficult set of choices—do I leave a job that's secure but aggravating? Do I end this relationship which was promising but is so filled with conflict?—parents may or may not be consulted, but they almost always have feelings and opinions. My boys gravitate toward wonderful partners. More than once, I've developed close and loving relationships with their girlfriends. Sometimes, they've broken up, and then I've mourned my loss, knowing it was my job to trust their decisions and focus on how much they grew in the course of the liaison.

settling in to adult-to-adult relationships

As the years go on and the lives of now fully-grown men and women become clearly defined, the emotional space for friendship ideally expands. But very often the physical space between the generations greatly expands, too. Modern societies demand a high degree of mobility. People follow jobs and careers and partners to distant places. No study of internal migration gives a more graphic picture of the situation than the nation's airports at holiday times.

I'm blessed to have my sons and their families live nearby. They do travel, sometimes frequently and far. As I wrote this chapter, Tuhin was in England visiting his in-laws and conducting business. He called and left a message on my voicemail: "Hi, Mom. Pat's dog has a HUGE tick on its chin. What's that old trick you used to do with a burned match to get ticks off?"

I can't tell you how gratified and how flattered I am that this executive of his own company, this respected man who is quoted in the press and consulted by legislators, still calls mom for advice on removing ticks.

part ii:
the stages

8

fertility and pregnancy:
new problems, new choices

Given a global crisis of over-population, there is irony that, in today's industrialized world, infertility is a problem to which enormous resources and scientific invention are turned.

In my practice, I have women getting pregnant the old-fashioned way. There are also a lesbian couple simultaneously inseminating with donations from each other's brothers; a straight couple dealing with the man's infertility through in vitro conception; a gay male couple adopting through a city program; and a single woman in her late forties going through the process of adopting a baby from abroad as a single parent. I've led women's groups in which everyone was dealing with issues of fertility in one way or another. Many of those would-be parents were older. Most did not get pregnant. It is a paradox that a technology of reproduction, both its inhibition and its enhancement, encouraged by women's political demands for control of their bodies and their life choices, has been complicit in producing a set of choices that are often painful in the extreme.

And the choices are legion. A *New York Times* headline reads: "Parenthood Is Redefined, but Custody Battles Remain Ugly" (6/12/04). The objects of the battle are twin boys conceived with father's sperm and, because mother was older (in fact, already had grown kids), donor eggs, carried by a surrogate mother, born after their never-married parents separated because the mother wanted to adopt a baby girl and the father objected. The mother then moved the twins from New York to California and, claiming domestic violence, sued for custody. The poor judge had to decide who or what was a parent before even considering the rights and wrongs of this particular case.

Although few are as complicated as in this story, there are many different reasons why conception today challenges the preconceptions of earlier generations. Fertility may be compromised for both men and women for reasons connected with life as we know it in industrial societies. Although men's fertility has suffered in modern times (likely culprits are pesticides and tight underwear), the most common cause is the greater age at which women, facing problems unique to the structure of today's working conditions, seek to conceive children. While more than half first-time moms in the United States are still in their twenties, over the last thirty years of the twentieth century, their average age rose just under four years to 25 years. That number represents a significant increase in birth mothers older than thirty. Texas, for instance, reported a 95.3 percent increase in the number of births to women over forty in the ten year period between 1986 and 1995.

There is a good deal of controversy over the relationship between age and fertility. One year the media is filled with stories urging women to hurry up and reproduce, the next to slow down and rely on medical interventions that are presented as near-infallible. Whichever story one chooses to believe, many people, male and female, opt to postpone parenthood until they've established economic security. For women, that means the business of building a career occupies the years of highest fertility.

I've said people "opt" for delayed parenthood, but the idea that such a choice is freely made is misleading. I've argued throughout this book that seemingly very personal decisions, in this case when to have a baby and with whom to do it, are in reality grounded in very impersonal dynamics. Social forces constrain and influence individual choice, especially if the factors involved go unrecognized. Once articulated, these processes still matter, but there is a far greater possibility of negotiating better options.

Let's look in more detail at what lies behind the choice to have babies later in life. During the second half of the twentieth century, the nature of women's participation in the labor market changed dramatically. Many women had worked for wages right along. Poorer families, especially families of color, depended on the earning power of women who worked in factories, as domestics, and at other low-wage jobs. But by the 1960s, forces were brewing that steered middle class women as well into the labor market. A new element, however, was the notion that these more affluent female workers would not simply hire out for wages, but would build careers. Traditions of working class white wives working briefly before or after childrearing, and of poorer women who held the same low-paying jobs throughout their adult lives, gave way to a different sense of life plan. Women of all heritages began to occupy higher rungs of the occupational ladder, professional and managerial positions. The wage gap between men and women began to diminish, although even now at 76 cents earned by women for a dollar earned by men, it still remains significant. A great deal of that reduced differential, however, was due not to women's successes but to men's hardships. By the 1980's, as highly paid unionized blue collar jobs left the country and union membership declined sharply, men's wage level sagged more quickly than women's increased.

One consequence of all these changes was to strain intimate relationships in unforeseen ways. The idea of the manly family breadwinner was often challenged, and with it the expectations of gender roles. Even when these crudest strains were absent, other dynamics appeared. Romantic ideals of relationship had more scope to play out as both men and women used the space between dating and birthing to seek partners who fulfilled multiple roles: lover, companion, friend, and, someday, co-parent. So many demands on relationships often led to disappointment, particularly because the focus on making such elaborate couples tended to compound a tendency for people to slight friendships and the maintenance of community in favor of their "squeeze." A woman may have been dating a man who she did not believe to be in the daddy league, or seeing someone younger than she who was not ready to start making babies. Having engaged in "serial monogamy," a string of relationships, satisfying or troubling, she may have grown increasingly insecure about her ability to build the kind of foundational connection she imagined to be a proper structure for parenting.

Suddenly finding herself in her mid or late thirties, many a working woman becomes frantic when she suddenly tunes in to the ever-louder ticking of the biological clock and realizes she's on track at work but badly side-tracked at home. More and more of my clients work feverishly trying to meet "Mr. Right," who now not only needs to be a great romancer but also an immediate daddy prospect. And the stakes get steadily higher as the years go on, and relationships become harder and harder to sustain. There's too much pressure, too much scrutiny, too little time to let nature take it's course. Women lose power in relationships, find themselves willing to do most anything to "make it work," and at the same time they often become increasingly angry at men who share neither their taste for nor their skill at "processing," the controversial business of talk, talk, talk that for many women is so essential to modern relationships. Feeling inadequate and criticized, men pull back. Women move proportionately forward and the dynamic gets worse and worse. Before they know it, these wannabe moms are mourning yet another ending, and finding themselves angry at men, self-recriminating, and confused.

For men, a parallel set of considerations exists. Domestic relationships are undergoing a transformation, and they are still in flux. In the past, couples were bound together by interdependencies, whether roles dictated by agricultural work, or small family crafts businesses, or in more modern times simply gender role divisions between work at home and work for wages. Women depended on men, as I've said, for money, and men depended on women for domestic and emotional labor.

But nowadays women have a good deal more financial mobility. They may have lower incomes and less job mobility as they care for children, but middle class women's need for men's wages is at least substantially diminished. Heterosexual women need men to produce children, and most prefer the partnership of raising them with spouses. But they have options they didn't have in past ages. Where does that leave men?

Often it leaves men in a quandary about their roles and responsibilities. If they don't "bring home the bacon," do they still get to "wear the pants"? What is the meaning of masculinity if the old model—strong and silent, hard-working in the labor force and therefore entitled to service at home—no longer holds? Not only are men no longer uniquely valued for their financial powers, but they are often pressured by women to participate in housework and childcare, and, even more confusingly, in a daily emotional dialogue.

Many men feel undervalued and underpowered. They aren't good at the things women demand of them, and they feel vaguely competitive about their mate's earning power. Wanting families as much as women do, they may run scared about their ability to measure up to women's standards. And so they both court women for relationships, and then withdraw from them as they hit walls of resentment over what they experience—behind mystifying veils of guilt—as unjust demands.

And so women find themselves running way behind their timelines for birthing children. Some decide to compromise in relationships, at least for now. Others find ways to get pregnant without surmounting the seemingly-impossible barrier of a "good relationship." Enter the fertility industry: sperm-banks, assisted fertility, surrogates and donors, and, year-by-year, more options.

going after pregnancy

Given the focused intention with which so many women and some men engage the business of baby-making, few potential parents do so without ambivalence. Don't give yourself a hard time because of it.

Along with the choice to postpone having babies, both men and women also come to believe that it is reasonable for them to make all sorts of choices about their lives: where to live, whether or not to stay close to their families of origin, when to change jobs and even careers. All this choice is bound up with a growing separation of individuals from collectivities. Young men and women are free to come and go, and mostly they go. Each life is conceptualized by the one who lives it as one; people come to see themselves as lone individuals entitled to autonomy. At the same time, this greater freedom involves significant losses, too: the loss of community, loss of intimacy. The search for partnership, for true love, the one and only, grows ever more intense.

So when the moment comes for such a securely formed individual to make the decision to bind herself or himself to a child, that prospect is complicated indeed. I commonly encourage prospective parents to articulate their fears, at the same time that they express their joy. The list is pretty predictable: I won't be able to come and go as I please anymore. I'll be trapped in a job I don't like for the sake of medical insurance or a basic wage. I'll be dirt poor; how will I afford all the costs of a family? I'll no longer be able to leave the relationship I'm in so freely, because divorce, however readily available, is a far weightier option once children's lives are affected. All these fears lie in the realm of the social. If we lived in a society that amply supported parents to raise children, then choice and mobility would not be constricted in the same ways. If community were an effective reality—with a battalion of aunts and uncles, whether inherited or intentionally chosen, standing at the ready to help, love, and support other people's kids—then the whole prospect of life-with-children would be very different indeed.

Beyond these socially-conditioned fears, there are the more primeval ones. What if something is wrong with my baby? Fear of disability is, I believe, also largely social in nature. That's a controversial claim, but I've learned over the years how much disability is (in the words of

Eleanor Smith, a wheelchair user who writes vividly about these issues) an oppression rather than a misfortune. Were we to be adequately cared for by society, whether we were "differently able" or not, if we lived in an economic culture that employed and valued people for the wide variety of contributions we can all make, then being "disabled" would simply mean being cared for in ways appropriate to that condition. Knowing, however, that care and advocacy will almost certainly fall to parents, with wholly inadequate social assistance, prospective parents are vulnerable to the bleeding of that fear into the more culturally inculcated terrors into which we are socialized in a society that values individuals according to productivity.

More primitive still than the fear of disability is a fear of dislike. What if this person I'm birthing is difficult or unlovable for some reason and just not a good fit for me? Think about the search for the perfect mate I've described, and especially about its frustrations; isn't it natural that we'd entertain fantasies of less-than-perfect relationships with offspring? On the other side of this particular coin are inscribed all those fears about whether you'll be the perfect parent you're supposed to be, if you are to qualify for relief from judgment, whether self and other-directed.

Despite all those qualms, if you're reading this book, you probably either have or are seriously planning to move forward. Here are some ideas about handling the business of getting pregnant outside of traditional means:

When to start fertility intervention: If you're female and with a male partner, the short answer is, not too soon. Standard advice is to wait a year of trying without fertility enhancement treatments. It often takes awhile for anything to happen. Think about the statistics: for a woman in her twenties, there is a 20-25 percent chance of conception during the few days each month that a woman is fertile. If you're in your thirties, that number goes down to about 15 percent (keeping in mind that there's an enormous range of fertility among women of

a given age). Assuming fertility were to be constant from one month
to another (which it's not, under the influence of all sorts of things
from nutrition to stress to who-knows-what), those odds repeat every
month. In other words, your chances do not get better in July because
you didn't get pregnant in May or June. So give statistics and nature a
really good chance. I know, it's disappointing to find yourself bleeding
month after month when you hoped to be pregnant. The pressure on
sex mounts, tempers grow thin; it's not much of a turn on.

The best advice I can give is easier said than done: relax and enjoy
it. Play games. Light candles. Go away to hot springs. This is your big
chance to have fun. Sure, other kinds of fun come with pregnancy and
babies. But infants do strain parents' sexuality. Maybe if you think of it
as among your last good times to indulge yourselves with utter freedom, you'll at least have mixed reactions when you find you haven't
conceived this time around.

Dealing with doctors: Medical personnel who specialize in fertility intervention are, no doubt, a fine and dedicated group of people.
But anecdotal evidence suggests they tend to come at their craft with,
perhaps, an overdose of scientism. That makes sense: they are the experts
at culling scientific knowledge and technique to the service of conception. But one corollary of a belief in the efficacy of science may be over
confidence in ones ability to predict outcomes. Earlier I mentioned
the therapy group wherein everyone was trying to get pregnant. Every
woman had, of course, had her hormone levels checked. The group was
punctuated with FSH (for Follicle Stimulating Hormone) numbers.
One reported a five, which is good; in her late thirties, her numbers
might have come from a woman ten years younger. Two were told that
they were marginal, unlikely to conceive without assistance, likely to
conceive with it. Two more with numbers higher than ten were told
that intercourse and/or insemination were not going to work. Their
particular factors strongly suggested IVF. Only one, Virginia, was told to
forget it. In fact, her doctor declared he didn't want to work with her

because it would be an exercise in disappointment for her and would reduce his success rate.

She was dashed but determined. In fact, she was angry. "How can he know with such certainty?!" she protested. Single at the time, Virginia presented her boyfriend with a proposition few men could resist: Get me pregnant and you can have the child in your life however you want, but I won't hold you responsible in any way, financial or parental. He readily agreed. Within two months, she was pregnant.

Finding the right approach for you: As with any medical procedure, it's wise to get several opinions. If you have insurance, find out what's covered, including second consultations. Check out Web sites to find reviews of available approaches. As I write, a good one I have encountered is called Fertility Plus (www.fertilityplus.org). It provides basic information about fertility and infertility written by lay people for patients. In general, the more information the better.

One question important to most people is cost. The price of fertility intervention is formidable. Most people I know who have succeeded in bearing kids that way have no later regrets. But think carefully about the money. To add enormous financial burdens to ones life can be stressful enough to threaten family unity. One couple in my practice mortgaged their house to do IVF (in-vitro fertilization). His sperm had zero motility, her FSH numbers were poor. They tried three times, each one gambling more money. No pregnancy resulted. As their money troubles grew, their marriage deteriorated.

A second significant consideration is physical. Most fertility intervention involves the use of heavy-duty hormones. Getting your body prepared for IVF, for instance, is not a picnic. Again, if a baby results, you're likely to forget the discomfort. But be prepared to deal with it while it's happening. One part of "dealing with it" falls to your partner, or whoever is around you on a detailed basis. Women get grumpy, not only because they are cramping or hyped up, but also because some of the reactions are emotionally fraught, a souped-up sort of PMS. In inverse proportion to the fun involved in the natural way of getting pregnant, IVF is not.

Now that I've detailed all the down parts of fertility intervention, I want to praise its merits. Many, many people who might otherwise have forgone the wild pleasure of bearing babies have benefited enormously from modern science. As with many hard things in life, choosing to go a medically-assisted route can clearly be the right choice. Once that fetus is growing within you, the rest fades to a dot on the horizon that you've just left.

Alternatives to medical infertility treatment: I know several stories of women who were told they would not conceive naturally and have nonetheless done it with the help of alternative treatments. None of these approaches has been tested with double-blind studies. What we have are anecdotes. I pass them along to you in that spirit. They may be things to try before going the more medical route, or they may not, depending on your sensibilities and pocketbook.

Virginia worked with an acupuncturist who focused on reproductive capacity. Susanna used homeopathy, which prescribes very minute quantities of a huge range of substances, highly refined, to stimulate the body's own healing potentials. After Martha's doctor diagnosed premature menopause, a healer suggested that the thirty-year-old try particular herbs such as Evening Primrose Oil. Her daughter Minna just graduated from high school.

Sometimes love can do it. Deborah, my dear friend, wanted nothing more than to have children when she found herself battling breast cancer in her early thirties. Although their marriage had been strained even before the diagnosis, Deborah's husband stood by her as she underwent surgery and draconian chemo therapy. When it was all done, her period was gone; she was told she'd never be able to have babies. Facing the daunting business of adoption, Deborah's husband bowed out of the marriage. She vowed to adopt as a single woman and started the long process of seeking a baby. Just as the letters "marketing" her as a prospective mom were ready to go out, Deborah met a man, a lovely man, Charley, who fell deeply in love with her. On the first date, she told him the worst: that she was a cancer survivor and that she was in the process of trying to adopt a baby. He put his head in his hands, wept, raised his head, and said, "So what!"

They were married soon afterward. Wisely, they decided to wait a year before trying to adopt, to give themselves time to build a strong foundation. About six months later, Deborah began to have troubling symptoms. Her remaining breast swelled. She started to gain weight unaccountably. She went to her doctor, terribly worried she was having some sort of recurrence of the cancer. He examined her and, in a flight of intuition, said, "Go to the lab down the street and get a pregnancy test."

It seemed a bad joke, and Deborah narrowly restrained herself from hitting him. After a vivid description of his insensitivity, she reluctantly let herself be persuaded. The result was negative; no pregnancy. She went back to her doctor. "Go back," he said. "Do it again." Again it was negative.

"OK," he said, "this time I'm sending you for a sonogram." And sure enough, there was a wiggly, heart-beating, heart-stopping fetus, four-month size! Deborah and Charley named her Mira for miracle.

So miracles do happen. But they can't be legislated. The next best thing is research—by you as well as by science—and perseverance.

When to stop trying: Giving up trying to get pregnant is an excruciating decision. Your money or your physical tolerance may have run out for the process. Or you may simply decide that the emotional travail is too stressful. So what next?

I believe you have several good choices. Adoption is the most obvious. I've found over the years that people have a range of intense feelings about adoption. For some, it is a wholly acceptable, maybe even a preferable route to a family. Some of the happiest stories of parenting I hear are by adoptive parents. There are, of course, risks involved. But it's a mistake to assume that natural childbirth doesn't also involve risks. On a relational level, making as clear a choice as possible to adopt is wise. I've written about the likelihood of ambivalence about starting out toward parenthood, so I don't expect contradictory feelings to suddenly vanish when it comes to adoption. But the process may take longer than nine months, and it may involve some challenges and disappointments along the way. Babies may appear as prospects and then be withdrawn. Foreign adoptions sometimes get scrambled up in politics or other international events. (Just as my brother and sister-in-law were eagerly ready to adopt Lucy from China, SARS hit and travel to China shut down. Then there was a trade show in their destination city and no hotels available. Then a national holiday slowed down the processing of visas. Once they finally got there and met Lucy, none of it mattered. But the wait was hard, hard, hard.) The worst of stories, of course, involve adoptions that are revoked after the baby and new parents have bonded. Heartbreaking though they are, these reversals do happen occasionally because biological parents who have relinquished a baby for adoption so often go through the tortures of ambivalence well after the fact.

Again, all those twists and turns of the road can strain relationships, although they can also bond partners in the unique way that adversity sometimes does. Along the way you don't have nine months of physical experience of a growing fetus to hook your engagement and focus your preparations. The process of getting to know an adopted baby and forming a new family around her or him may be delicious or complex; for sure your process will be your own and unlike anyone else's.

The methods of finding a baby to adopt have expanded over the years. Starting with the simplest, Mamie and Veronica were just beginning to consider a baby when a close friend, who knew they were talking about it, called to say her teen-aged cousin in Nebraska was about to give birth and had decided to give the baby up for adoption; would they like her? Two weeks later, they were on a plane returning home with a baby. Their friends surprised them with a crib and layette, for they'd barely had time to arrange time off from work not to mention preparing for an infant's arrival.

A more modern form of word-of-mouth involves lawyers and promotional materials. This approach is the one Deborah had been prepared to use before meeting Charley. She found a lawyer in the business of seeking babies, who coached her to prepare a letter about herself, expounding her many potential virtues as a mom. She included photographs of herself, her house, the baby's room, the grandmother. She had hundreds of copies made of the whole glossy packet.

In the black community, and many others as well, informal extended family adoption is very common. The subject of cross-racial adoption is controversial. White parents adopting African-American babies confront deep and constant demands to deal with the issues of racism particular to black people in the United States. Some of these dynamics are similar to those with foreign adoptions, but the history of slavery and the particularly complex and oppressive relations between white and black Americans are also unique. No wonder that many African-American people strongly prefer that babies go to black homes. If white parents do adopt across these racial lines, I strongly advocate that they seek active support from other adoptive parents and from wise souls in the African-American community. This is an arena in which humility is crucial. Know that there is much you cannot know about the experience of racism, and seek people from whom you can learn it long before you find yourself unable to help your child negotiate that troubled territory.

9

discipline and punishment
relying on relationship,
not retaliation

So far in this book, I've used the word "discipline" more often to advise
an inward-bound action rather than an outward one. That is, more than
once I've counseled you as a parent to discipline your own reactions
and programmed beliefs as opposed to disciplining your child's behavior. Discipline, in this sense, is about a kind of self-control that allows
time to reflect on one's own behavior and to choose a course of action
based on thoughtfulness and information.

Isn't that precisely the sequence you wish your child to follow?

Punishment is an act of coercion designed to impose on another
person your own choice of options. It is a power play, a use of superior
force for the purpose of compelling someone to do what you want.
Power plays and power-sharing are polar opposites; one precludes the
other.

If you've been reading right along in this book, it will come as no
surprise that I'm a strong advocate of self-discipline without punishment, for both children and parents.

Let's look at both sides of that coin. How you might punish your
child is pretty clear. On a range from the most overt forms—physical
acts of spanking, beating, or otherwise inflicting pain—to the most covert forms—the willful withholding of affection or other resources—a
menu of parental punishments is not hard to write. With the exception

of affection, the means available to parents for imposing their will on children are asymmetrical: children cannot beat parents (not with very much effectiveness, at least until they reach a certain size), withhold allowances, impose "groundings," send adults to their room, and so on. Parents, in other words, have more power to punish kids than the other way around.

Nonetheless, the difference between a constructive use of power and a power play is not always obvious. Are there times when parents' greater wisdom advises the wielding of their greater power through punishment?

At the risk of appearing extreme, I would say no. That is not to say that the use of greater physical strength is not sometimes wise. If your child is running into traffic, by all means restrain her.

But short of an emergency, there are usually alternatives. When Jesse was of crawling age, we went camping in a large group. Jesse was seeing fire for the first time, and he wanted it! We barricaded the campfire with large logs and whatever else we could find, but Jesse was a determined lad and kept climbing over them. Finally, I took Jesse to the fire and bit by bit I held his hand closer and closer. Each time I thought he could feel the heat, I'd say, "Hot!" and pull his hand dramatically away. The baby laughed, and I moved a little closer, until finally he began pulling his own hand away and saying his version of "Hot!" He stayed away from the fire from then on.

Some time back, punishment fell out of favor. Experts (and soon afterward, parents) began to speak instead of "setting limits" (witness Sencia's dads) and of "consequences." These notions have validity, but only when the limits and the consequences are real, not willful choices on the part of a person with the power to impose them. If I have to get to work at a certain time, that's a genuine limitation on my child's ability to be slow getting ready in the morning. If I'm exhausted at the end of the day, my fatigue is a real limit to my willingness, perhaps my physical ability, to rough-house with my kindergartner.

If my child refuses to go to bed at the appointed time, the real consequence is not a loss of some desired privilege the next day but rather
a cranky child and exhausted parent. To create a "consequence" is to
engage in a battle. To name a natural consequence is to offer choice to
a child. One area of genuine consequence is emotional; my despair at a
delayed bedtime is probably real and not invented.

But what if I express that despair through a temper tantrum? Emotional honesty is a good thing. But there is a skill involved. A client of
mine related the following story: Her four-year-old had started hitting
her, a return to an earlier behavior she'd seemed to have outgrown.
Before, her mom had introduced ideas of gentler emotional expression.
"You can say you're angry without hitting, you know." Pretty soon, the
little girl had adopted that strategy.

Now, however, she was hitting with a vengeance, strong punches
landing on mom's stomach. They hurt. After several attempts at reason,
Mom said in an intense voice, "Ouch!! That really hurt. I don't think
I want to hang out with you right now if you're going to hit me." She
went to her room and began to read a book.

I asked if she were play-acting, or if her departure was a truthful
expression of what she felt. She said that what had alarmed her was that
she really did feel detached from her daughter, a child she ordinarily
adored. She badly needed some time to recover and feel love again.

After a bit, the child came into the room and leaned against her. "I'll
want to be with you again soon, I'm sure," her mom said. "But I'm still
not ready. I'm still feeling hurt, and pretty angry, too."

The little girl left the room and came back shortly with a picture
of a weeping face. "Are you sad?" she asked. Mom said she was. "I don't
want to feel angry at you. That makes me sad."

The daughter left and came back in a few minutes with another
picture of a laughing face. "Will you be happy again?" she asked. "Yes,
I'm sure I will be."

A third time, the child came back with a drawing of a heart with a smiling face inside. "Now, Mommy?" she asked. "Yes, now," said her mother, heart warming, and she returned to playing.

I thought the exchange demonstrated something very powerful about both mother's and daughter's exercise of emotional power, a shared process. My client might have punished her child by turning coldly away from her, threatening her with a withdrawal of love. Instead, she engaged her daughter honestly, staying true to the real consequences of the child's hitting. It was a demonstration of something natural: if you are violent to another person, you won't get love and attention in return. The same act of withdrawal might have been contrived. Instead, the mom's behavior grew from an intention to express her feelings rather than to coerce her daughter into stopping a detrimental action. The child might dislike the real consequence of her hitting, but she could not quarrel with her mother about it. To be real might invite protest against the natural world, but it did not engage mother and daughter in battle with each other. Instead, the mother expressed something in act and word that happened, in the end, to mirror exactly the path she hoped her daughter might discover when she, too, felt something disagreeable.

All I could add, besides applause, was the suggestion that they talk about it later. "I wonder what she was feeling and wanting when she hit you," I questioned. "Given your daughter's level of emotional skill, I bet she can tell you." To return to a confrontation in the calm of the aftermath is an opportunity for both parent and child to deepen understanding and to imagine greater possibilities.

yes, but...

"What if what I'm honestly feeling is that I'm sick and tired of negotiating and just want the kid to do what I want—especially since I know a whole lot more about what he *should* do!" Jesse's father exclaimed one day. In a sentence, he summed up the difficulty of abjuring punishment. It is giving up something substantial. Sometimes life just doesn't offer up enough time and energy (which equals people) for a no-punishment policy to be realistic.

And what about authority, the kind of wisdom that comes of life experience? Doesn't good parenting include bestowing the benefit of an adult's greater knowledge on kids in order to protect them from at least some of life's harder lessons?

Exasperation, impatience, and hurt feelings are all a part of parenting, I'm afraid. To say those things to a child is fine. Like dogs that watch their humans for signs of the emotional weather, kids are similarly attuned to adults' emotions, spoken or unspoken. Now and then, I'm sure Jesse's dad echoed a famous advertising slogan, "Jesse, just do it. We can talk about it later, but right now, just do it!"

But I'm equally sure that Jesse knew with certainty that his dad respected him, would love him no matter what, and at another moment would stop and reflect if Jesse were to reply, "Why?"

Yes, it's harder to parent without authoritarianism. That doesn't mean giving up authority, however, which is a very different matter. Authority is about what I know; authoritarianism is about imposing what I know on others through intimidation, without discussion.

If it's harder at this stage, though, it's a whole lot easier later on. Jesse was a model teenager. He was not exactly quiet; in fact, he became a youth leader in the community. He challenged his parents in ways that educated them to new thinking about the world. But he remained adorable, loving, creative, articulate—himself, in short—throughout.

The discipline that children who are not punished learn is a product of integrity. Out of self-knowledge and an assumption of their ability, and right, to self-determine, they do what is right for them. They may make mistakes, but within bounds of sanity. One of my learning moments was a day when Tuhin and I were hiking along the edge of a cliff along the Pacific coast. I'm fairly fearless, but my one panic button is kids around sheer drops. "Be careful!" I kept shouting as Tuhin, a physical and joyful seven-year-old at the time, frolicked along the trail.

At last he stopped and turned to me. "Mom," he said, reason dripping from his voice, "do you really think I want to fall off the cliff any more than you want me to? I promise I won't leap over the edge. Chill."

Clearly, what I knew about reason and communication had taken hold in Tuhin. Relaxation was not immediate, but thereafter, in many circumstances, I remembered that conversation and could manage my anxieties, coming closer and closer to a state of "chill."

upping the ante in teenage years

How much of adolescent behavior is shaped by rebellion against restrictions experienced earlier in life! First we Rescue kids, conveying to them through things done for them and to them that they don't have the good sense to sort things out for themselves. Then we try to control them when they reach an age of relative liberation and for the first time have the freedom to make their own mistakes. Meanwhile, they've moved to Persecution, expressed as an intolerance for everything adults think they know and seek to impose.

To give up punishment at this stage is truly difficult.

On the other hand, the menu of possible punishments shrinks dramatically when kids reach the point of autonomous movement through the world outside the home. You can ground a kid, but are you around at the relevant times to police the order? You can withhold money, but you may begin to notice the odd twenty-dollar bill missing from your wallet. You can refuse the keys to the car, but do you really prefer your teenager being driven by some kid you know little or nothing about?

Do you want to be cop to your child's criminal act for the next four years?

"Start early" is good advice, but not if you're reading this book with a fifteen-year old rebel in your home. No wonder teenage boot camps have become a boom industry!

"Tough love" is a trademarked system for taming wild children, especially popular with parents of older kids. Over the years, I've seen desperate parents turn to handbooks and coaches drawing on a tough love approach. For some, it's offered a modicum of relief; for others, it's escalated an even tougher war.

One piece of tough-love advice with which I agree is to pick your battles. Having chosen those things that are most important to you—can you give up a neat room in return for greater assurance that your teenager won't drink and drive?—then negotiate clear and concrete agreements on the subject. What will you do if you slip and have a drink at a party when you're the designated driver? Does the commitment include not getting in a car with a driver who's been drinking? What about pot; is it as hazardous to driving ability as alcohol? (I'll write more about problems involving substances in the next chapter.)

"Tough love" can mean simply being really, really true to what you feel and want as you negotiate with your child. Or it can be a mandate to come down hard at the earliest sign of trouble. Proportion is, I believe, everything in this arena. Overreaction is as dangerous to your teenager's well-being as under-reaction; probably more so, because you're relating to a person who is intent on self-definition. Also, he or she may not trust you. If you've been on the see-saw between power-sharing and punishment in the past, your word in a negotiation now may seem less that golden. You may need to overcome a credibility problem. Being self-critical about the times in the past when you've said one thing but done another (and who among us is entirely innocent?) is a step forward. Admit your mistakes and claim your lessons openly and verbally with your child. Then be very, very clear about what the change is that you're seeking to institute now.

It's not a bad idea to ask your teenager to tell you if she or he thinks you're repeating past mistakes now. Be open, like Jesse's parents, to being student to your kid as well as guide and teacher.

Turning the corner side-by-side with an adolescent often requires some special structures for dialogue, ways of talking that dramatize the idea of moving in a new direction. I always found that conversations while driving were helpful; you and your kid can sit side-by-side, making eye contact only when chosen. Long gaps of silence, while awkward indoors, are unremarkable in a moving vehicle.

Finding a mediator may be the next step in intensifying the conversation. I do many of these sessions with parents and teenagers, and I love them because they are so productive. A friend or relative can play that role as well. One of my most memorable conversations with Tuhin about his grievances over some of my life choices happened while we were visiting an old friend in New Delhi. She was able to listen with enormous compassion for both of us. Moreover, having been present (and a guide) while I made some of those choices, she was able to fill in blanks in Tuhin's knowledge about the circumstances and possibilities. Coming from me, those same statements might have sounded (and probably been) defensive. From her, they were loving and informative.

10

substance abuse:
when to intervene

Throughout this book, I've advocated for clear and open dialogue. But what if you have the strong suspicion that you're dealing with a creature who is not capable of rational negotiation? What if you fear that your child is addicted to drugs or alcohol?

For most parents, at the end of the day doubt is more the problem than substances. Up until now, you may have felt you had a pretty good grip on understanding your child. But your adolescent's sudden changes in behavior are subject to question. Is this just a normal process of the kid's defining himself as separate from you? Is she rebelling in ways that don't make much sense beyond the raw fact of rebellion?

Or is something more sinister going on?

Many parenting guides on the subject list warning signs: abrupt change in grades, playing hooky, money missing from mom's purse, unexplained hostility and secrecy, and so on. The problem is that all these actions could be explained in a number of different ways.

Besides, these are the years for experimentation in all sorts of ways, substance use included. When does use become abuse? How can you judge where the dividing line lies? And can you trust your teenager to be asking those same questions, not to mention coming up with good answers?

Some of your confusion may derive from your own history of experimentation with drugs and alcohol. Unless you grew up in a strict religious community that forbade such practices, you can probably hark back to a time when you were drunk or stoned. Maybe you even tried harder stuff; maybe you struggled to control your usage or maybe you decided pretty quickly you didn't like the sensations associated with types or degrees of use and gave it up.

I often hear parents say things like, "Well, yeah, sure I used at her age. But the pot was less potent in those days. Nowadays, it's *really* dangerous!"

It's a bit harder to claim that booze has gotten more virulent, but parents may similarly downplay their own adolescent use and live in terror of their teen's.

For those parents who are children of the sixties, these issues are especially complex and confusing. Many have been reasonably open with their kids about their wild times. They may have expressed values of openness to consciousness-changing experience while somehow never quite imagining how they'd feel when their own kids actually mirrored the parents' experimentation. Some may today smoke dope on a regular basis or be loathe to give up the evening cocktail (or two or three) or half-bottle of wine with dinner.

Once more, establishing policy with children forces parents to examine their own behaviors and assumptions. Do I have a problem with substances? Is it possible I need to cool it? Or is it true that, somehow, I can handle it but my son or daughter of sixteen can't?

Once more, fear shades many parental reactions in tones of shocking pink, making it harder to maintain a reasoned dialogue with the child. It may be that you are as incapable of rational dialogue as your suspected-to-be-chemically-altered teenager.

checking for problems

Definitions of substance abuse are hazy and subject to argument. I prefer a strategy that asks a different question: What are the problems associated with my use of alcohol or other mind-altering substances? There are three typical categories of problems that arise, assessed by three reasonably straight-forward questions:

- **Is my use hurting my body?** Do I black out while drinking? Do I wake up hung-over? Do I have chronic sinus inflammation from smoking? Am I exposing myself to disease by using needles?
- **Is my use hurting my relationships?** Are those I care about having to guess what state I'm in at any given moment? Am I being secretive or do others suspect me of dishonesty? Am I alienating loved ones by being altered when they are not? Am I missing times to be with people whose company I value because I'm using substances instead?
- **Is my use out of my control?** Can I decide I'm only going to have one drink tonight and stick to it? Can I make a plan to smoke dope only rarely and only at a social event? Am I faithful to my vow never to drive when drinking and only to be in a car with someone who has had nothing to drink?

You'll notice that I phrased the questions in the first person singular. Inquiry is most helpful when it's self-reflection, by you or by your teenager.

What do you do, though, when your child is protesting innocence and you're not convinced? The guidelines remain the same as they were earlier in your career as a parent: Be on your kid's side, not on his or her case. Speak frankly but in terms of your worries and concerns. Talk personally.

Still, a person who is seriously chemical addicted may well lie and do it convincingly. How can you judge your child's truthfulness? On one level, persistent lying tends to become known over time. It is very hard to maintain a consistent story. Ask about contradictions you hear, not in a spirit of inquisition but as a quest for trust. Truthfulness is a two-way street; be honest about your distress and you may elicit honesty in return.

But at some point if reality does not add up, your anxieties may reach a breaking point. I work with a theory about truth-telling that challenges psychiatric definitions of paranoia. Rather than pathology, I see the fearful construction of alternative realities as a sign of mental health. Human beings are at our core truth-seekers. That is all the more true when the well-being of one's child is in question. In this perspective, paranoia can be seen as heightened awareness, as intuition informed and made intense by need to make sense of something important but unspoken. Such intuition is often both accurate and inaccurate. It grows from a kernel of truth, from some non-verbal piece of information – a turn of the head, a downward glance, a discrepancy between expectation and actuality. But if the kernel of truth can't be securely identified, then we invent stories to account for what we intuit. The less we know for sure, the more we create explanations, and more and more distortion is likely to creep in. Powerlessness is a strong propellant in the direction of paranoia. The less able I am to get the truth I need, the less able I am to protect myself from a feared danger, the more I grasp for the information I need and the more my powers of invention become engaged.

Issues of substance abuse and teenagers provide a recipe for paranoia. Kids, fearful of parents' impulse to control them at a time when they seek ever greater freedom, interpret benign parental acts as outrages. Parents, unable to judge accurately their teenager's good judgment, find their imaginations fueled by fear to distressing levels. When the subject is drugs, a problem-area exploited by popular culture and modeled by celebrities of teen culture, paranoia is likely to be at its highest pitch.

It is an act of supreme alliance to validate a paranoia honestly, and then to correct any inaccuracies. Lacking validation, reassurance rings hollow. We've all had the experience of saying over and over, "No, no, I still love you," to a paranoid partner. As irritation grows at the futility of the repeated conversation, the words come increasingly to contradict their emotional content. But if you can first say, "Well, what's true is that I'm angry at you right now for not doing the dishes, but I still love you dearly," you're more likely to get a satisfying hearing. The kernel of truth may be that your attention is wandering from the relationship, that you're distracted right now by problems of your own, even that you're troubled by an attraction to someone at work but have zero intention to act on it. The harder the content of the truth, the more likely you are to omit it, to jump clear over a piece of information that might be hard for your partner to hear (or scary for you to confess). As long as it remains unsaid, though, there is a breach in your emotional connection, and it is likely to grow larger over time. In the absence of knowledge we all tend to substitute our worst fears. The demons come out of the closet; only knowing for sure what's what can render them harmless once again.

This dynamic is at the very heart of many families' experiences around issues of teen substance use. To speak the truth is an act of compassion and commitment, and those states of feeling are more likely between young people and parents when their relationship is essentially positive.

In my story about Adam and Bettina, the dialogue about Bettina's worries turned in a constructive direction when mother and son had dealt with other causes for estrangement between them. To the extent that you and your teenager are negotiating the intense changes of this period as allies, you'll have more or less success questioning drug and alcohol use.

Bettina elicited more sympathy from Adam when she related her fears to her brother's death from a drug overdose. When Adam could hear what she asked of him not as a bid to control him but as a request for his help reassuring her, he was more forthcoming.

when the worst fear is true

Adam may have been handling chemicals well enough to restore trust, but what of the youngster who is not? What do you do if you become convinced that your offspring does have a serious problem with drugs or alcohol?

First, I want to address the emotional environment surrounding these issues. We live in a moral climate of extreme censoriousness toward addiction. Western industrial society demands a large load of self-control of its denizens. Strength of character is often judged by one's capacity for self-denial. We are intolerant of over-eaters, over-consumers, over-users of chemicals—of over-just-about-everything except over-workers. The latter is valorized, all the former demonized.

That, I believe, is why the Twelve Step programs insist that addiction is a disease. If you have an inherited disorder, you are not morally responsible for the consequences. You may still have to develop means to control addictive behavior, but the inclination to over-indulge is not about your will; it resides in your genes.

Together, moral and medical explanations of addiction crowd out social understandings. How many of us eat or drink or smoke or swallow prescription drugs because we don't know what else to do to relieve the stress and human alienation that result from our over-busy, insecure, and isolated lives? Once upon a time, stopping at the local smoke-filled bar for a drink was (reasonably) an acceptable way to transition from work to home (with a gender tilt, of course, advantaging men). Gathering around alcohol still often structures socializing. Meanwhile, particular groups of people form shared identities by the use of certain drugs--marijuana, Ecstasy, cocaine, and crack: each substance is often associated with a different segment of the population.

Little wonder, then, that teenagers, intent on forming new peer worlds with the smallest possible interaction with adults, would be drawn toward chemical bonds. If dad was an "alcoholic," it does not necessarily mean that the son has the "alcoholic gene." It may more mean that the family has few other traditions for comfort and connection. Family cultures are strong and persistent, and mostly they reflect elements from the larger culture in which families reside. To flatten these complex histories, embodying meaningful but harmful strategies for solving genuine problems, into either moral failings or medical diagnoses is a distinct disservice to the needs underlying the problems.

So step one in confronting a child's misuse of substances is to manage your fears and disarm your moral judgments.

Having done so, the next step is to open a supportive and honest dialogue with the child: "I'm seriously concerned about how you're using alcohol/pot/etc.," rather than, "I know you're an addict and need to be locked into treatment!"

"I really want and need to have an honest conversation with you; please, please level with me," not, "How could you be so stupid as to let yourself get out of control?!"

Demonstrate your understanding of the reasons why the teen might be in trouble with substances. Express your belief that this is the time for experimentation leading to a healthy relationship with whatever chemical is at issue. Civilizations have used an enormous variety of mind-altering plants and brews for purposes of celebration, spiritual journeying, and pleasure. Allow the possibility that today's young people can find a balance that allows for positive use rather than abuse.

For the greatest number of families, staying in this dialogue will prove sufficient. Most of us are not addicts (despite popular culture's distortions to the contrary). Most young people move through a mishap or two on the way to making sound decisions about their relationship to substances. Here above all is a place for supportive guidance rather than misguided control.

the exception that proves the rule

Nonetheless, a small minority of youngsters may be chemically addicted to something that they can't control. That hard core of reality often promotes an overblown reaction to the majority that it does not describe. But if it becomes clear over time that it is true for your youngster, what then?

Treatment programs abound these days. Just as the alcohol industry is a huge profit-maker, so too are organizations dedicated to intervention. Too many treatment programs resort to draconian means, infused, I believe, with all the moral outrage that our discipline-oriented society levels at both addicts and adolescents. If you find yourself dealing with an angry, chemically altered, rebellious, death-defying teenager, a punitive lock-down may seem just the ticket. Indeed, "tough love" programs that spirit teenagers away in the dead of night and ship them off to desert boot-camps may produce results. But there are (at least) two problems: They may produce even more rebellion, cementing teenage behavior into a life-long identity. And they may accomplish submission through terror that creates adults who white-knuckle adherence to values that trap them in unsatisfying lifestyles. Finding a path in life that is right for each of us takes a good deal of self-knowledge and will to step outside prescribed lines of development. Fearful obedience to someone else's rules is the antithesis of the mindset needed to remain open to possibilities.

Pursuing a critique of her own experience in one such rehab program, author Maia Szalavitz interviewed over a hundred people who had either been to a similar one or sent their child to one. These harsh residential facilities share a philosophy that addicts must be torn down before they can reconstruct a drug-free persona. Maia disputes the underlying premise. "I took drugs compulsively," she writes in a newspaper column, "The Trouble with Tough Love", "because I hated myself." Convinced that no one who truly knew her could love her, she masked her depression by socializing through the auspices of drugs. Once drug-free and in the confines of a confrontational rehab program, she suffered raw emotional pain without relief.

"Why would being humiliated, once I'd given up the only thing that allowed me to feel safe emotionally, make me better?" she asks. "My problem wasn't that I needed to be cut down to size; it was that I felt I didn't measure up."

Mariah Breeding, a drug counselor for many years who for a time headed an adolescent treatment program, remarked that Maia's pattern was especially true for girls. "I can't think of one girl I treated who didn't deal with a sense of self-contempt."

I'm not so sure that boys fare very much better. What may be true is that ideas of masculinity provide them with more rigid character structures within which to defend their addictive behaviors, as well as their rebellions. The problem, then, isn't so much about substances as it is about a relationship with self and society.

I can't offer very helpful advice about finding humane help if you conclude that your teen needs professional intervention. Keep shopping. Interview the program leadership in detail about their approach. Use your keenest intuition—your well-placed paranoia—to choose the most compassionate, non-judgmental, supportive counselors you can find. Above all, don't give up on your child. This, like life, is a point along a path. It is not a definition of character nor a prediction about the future. Dealing with addiction is a thing in the present, and it is at its very heart a struggle for human comfort and close connection. Your job as parent is to do your very best to stay attuned to those needs, your own as well as your child's.

11

divorce:
"nobody asked what i want!"

Sharing power has its limits, and one big one is the decision of parents to separate. While people often stay together "for the sake of the children," that choice rarely involves a family vote.

Josh was four when his parents broke up. After the dust had settled, we asked him how he was feeling and a cascade of tears began to fall. At length he looked up through his long eyelashes and said, "I'm really sad. Nobody asked me what I want."

It came as a revelation to us how unusual that was. We were always asking Josh what he wanted, up until now.

We validated his perception. "It's true. There are some things kids don't get a choice about. This is one of them."

We went on to sort out in some detail where he did have the power of choice and where he did not: He could enter into negotiations about schedules and activities, but he had no real voice in deciding whether or not his parents lived in the same home. He could join with his dad to furnish and decorate a room in his house, and his dad was even fine with house-hunting with Josh so that he could voice opinions about where he wanted to live when he was with his father. But the range of choices of homes was limited by finances.

Once again, everybody's needs and rights were equal, but Josh had less power in many realms. To acknowledge those limitations in the specific was at least to give him the power of information.

Josh's parents were committed to negotiations like these, with him and with each other. Within a year, Josh was discovering some distinct advantages of a two-household family: two rooms to mess up, two times in a week to do fun things with a parent, two groups of friends with kids, and so on.

People often regard divorce as failure. We're supposed to make relationships "work." If we don't, we "break up." Afterward, we need to "heal." Language follows culture, and this culture has a very strong bias in favor of lifelong commitments, a distinct contradiction with reality in a time when half of all couples married today will (according to Census Bureau predictions) someday divorce. Once upon a time, "till death do us part" was functional. As I've written in an earlier chapter, marriage was an institution designed to provide for the care of children, financial protection for women (at least on a legal basis), and rights to patriarchal authority for men. Marriages linked people to extended kinship networks; families were also economic entities, working farm or shop or small manufactory together.

By the early twentieth century, the character of husband-wife relationships had changed; a majority of American families were supported by wage labor, and the functionality of families shifted. If one partner worked (usually a man) and the other stayed home, the wage earner depended on the care of a wife, while the wife needed the economic support of a wage earner. This division of labor—money for nurturance, domesticity for worldliness—created mutual dependency. Infidelity may have been common, unhappiness familiar, but divorce was rare.

But in the 1960s and thereafter, another major change set in. As more and more middle class women joined their working class sisters in the job market, the strains of personal life increased (nobody home to make the dinner and raise the kids) at the same time that the need for women to stay in unhappy marriages decreased (two-paycheck families may still have been financially strapped, but women had far more economic mobility than had their mothers.)

In these changed circumstances, absent a moral charge, divorce becomes a viable choice. I often think of relationship, like parenting, as being a developmental process. An ideal intimacy before the advent of children—replete with romance, friendship, adventure—may be truly irritating after the birth of babies. What people need at that stage of life is a working partnership grounded in some very strong confluences of values and beliefs about child rearing. After kids have grown into some degree of independence, however, partners may seek yet other functions for their intimacy—perhaps an inclination toward shared spiritual growth, travel, or a companionship based in creative interaction.

Some partners manage to grow in tandem, to change and enrich their relationship several times in the course of decades. But in other cases people develop in ways that stretch the malleability of a relationship too far for practicality. If one partner wants to travel and another to start a small business, if one discovers a new well of sexuality while the other craves estheticism, compromise may do a disservice to both. To part when needs and wants change, to be willing to move on is not a sign of failure but, often, of courage. If we can do it in this spirit, then partings may be full of gratitude and friendship rather than recrimination and shame. Sadness, a recognition of loss, the pain of reconstruction: these feelings are based in fact. But blame is usually a product of ideas, of expectations unmet, and of judgments inherited from external sources.

I'm not arguing that divorce should be undertaken lightly; despite certain media portrayals, I've yet to see a blithe divorce. Then too, some partings might be avoided if people knew better how to work things out, which I believe translates into, if people had more help from a wider community. When break-ups happen while people are still engaged in parenting, they are especially difficult. Parents make choices to alter lives beyond their own, and most often they do so with deep consideration and worry.

You don't have to look hard to find two very different literatures on the effects of divorce on kids. One expert says it's devastating, another says it's not. My perception over the years is that there are two conditions that make the difference between these outcomes: degree of financial well-being and quality of cooperation between the divorced parents.

First, poverty makes a difference. In the 1980's there began to appear research on what was called "the feminization of poverty." As divorce rates climbed, the financial well-being of single women with children plummeted. The phenomenon was not hard to understand, on a statistical level. In 1980 women earned around sixty cents to men's dollar. Child support payments rarely made up the gap between the statistically average dad's income and mom's. Even where formal payments seemed adequate, where childcare was agreed to be fifty-fifty, it turned out that women spent a significantly greater amount of time with children and spent a significantly larger amount of money on things like clothing and incidentals. These economic results were not caused by male stinginess or meanness. They were an aggregate phenomenon of many small, often-unnoticed inequalities between the sexes that added up to heightened prosperity for divorced men and distinct poverty for divorced women with children.

Today's statistics are slightly less extreme, but not by a whole lot. Today, the gender wage gap has narrowed to about seventy-six cents. More women earn higher salaries (although in some of the highest categories—physicians, for instance—women are still underrepresented at 31% and earn only 58% of men's income), but, as I mentioned earlier, some economists claim that the major portion of the change in the wage ratio is due to a decline in men's earning power rather than an increase in women's. As higher paid blue collar jobs have vanished along with American heavy industry and labor union membership, men are faring significantly worse financially as women fare a little better.

the good divorce

What are the consequences for children of divorce? Judith Wallerstein is a sociologist who published alarming research about the psychological devastation kids suffered after parents separated. But it turned out that Wallerstein had studied families in affluent Marin County, just north of San Francisco. Marin is largely a bedroom community. At the time, the family wage earner tended to commute to the city to a highly-paid job. Left at home in the suburbs after the divorce, with rusty job skills and a determination to spend as much time as possible with their kids, mothers had a hard time finding any but poorly paid local work. The feminization of poverty set in, big time.

Wallerstein found that children were disoriented, alienated from their peers, depressed.

Other researchers, Terry Arendell and Demie Kurz among others, observed quite different consequences. While mothers struggled with hard problems, there were no discernable ill effects on children beyond transitory ones in the immediate aftermath of a parent's departure. Some positive effects were a greater degree of participation in home life by kids, richer relationships between children and divorced dads, more emotional communication among family members in general.

In today's world, commonly both mothers and fathers work to make ends meet. There is little enough disposable income around to smooth the way in a divorce. I see the results of that reality often in my practice. Inadequate funding is a source of tension, combining with other emotional wounds in a stew of ongoing conflict. If both parents face endless labor, debt, insecurity, and competitiveness for scarce resources, it is very hard to work through other issues amicably—childcare arrangements and childrearing philosophies and vacation schedules and educational decisions are among the most typical. All of which is not to say that people don't manage; I'm often moved by how ingeniously and bravely people deal with financial, as well as most other, problems.

The second condition for protecting kids from harm after a divorce, cooperation, is, I believe, at least as important. All the post-separation issues that lead to disharmony I've just mentioned constitute exactly the same impasses that often cause people to give up on a relationship in the first place. It is a paradox that divorce is often the result of parents' inability to work together in a collaborative way, yet separating and establishing new households and arrangements call for a high degree of collaborative problem solving. If people had been able to negotiate successfully right along, they might still be together.

Sometimes, a couple breaks up for other reasons: a breach in trust involving another sexual entanglement, a mid-life crisis that prompts one partner to seek new love, a hot job offer in a city the spouse can't abide, a discovery of a change in sexual orientation. Very rarely I come across a couple who have mutually decided their lives would benefit from an end to the marriage or partnership. But much more often a breakup involves anger, grief, shock, disorientation, and the extreme stress of putting together new households and constructing new social lives.

Under these circumstances, how hard it is to accomplish an amicable and cooperative separation! Yet the less animosity there is between parents, the more likelihood there is that the change will benefit rather than harm the children. I have worked with many an adult with divorced parents who, in retrospect, report their relief when they realized they were free of the constant conflict between the adults. Divorce may be sad and confusing for children, but so is living in a household filled to the brim with grown up tension—in some families, tension that bursts into periodic violence. To gain the advantages of peace at home as soon as possible, a well-mediated divorce is enormously helpful. Here are two examples from my mediation practice:

mediating divorce, mediating pain

Jemaine and Gayle were a couple for fifteen years. They separated when a long accumulation of resentment tipped Jemaine over the edge and she decided she wanted to end the relationship. They had three children, a ten-year-old son and twin girls, just turned six at the time of the separation.

When they came to mediation, they were still living together. It took very little exploration to convince me that they were beyond reconciliation. They'd been in couples counseling for long enough that Jemaine was sure she was done and Gayle, heartbroken though she was, had accepted the inevitable.

Our first order of business was to find a way for them to have enough physical distance from each other that they could begin the reconstruction. Gayle was so sad and angry, and she felt so powerless that hard feelings radiated from her expressive body language even when she determined to say nothing. Jemaine, in reaction, was steely. For her, feeling was not possible so long as she was witnessing Gayle's pain on a daily basis. Guilt and anger cycled in rapid succession, and she resisted both while struggling to maintain her resolve. The children hadn't been told yet that their mothers were separating, but both women knew they were reading the winds and bearing up with fear just under the surface.

Gayle came from a wealthy family, and she herself was a professional who earned a sizable salary. Jemaine had very little; working for a non-profit social service organization would never make her rich. Of European heritage, Gayle had learned through her relationship with Jemaine, whose father was African American and mother white, an awareness of the differences in their race-associated experiences in a discriminatory society. Despite her profound feelings about the end of their relationship, Gayle quickly declared her intention to provide for Jemaine, out of love for her soon-to-be-ex partner and because she understood so clearly the advantage to the children.

Jemaine agreed to find an apartment right away, and they made a plan to take turns staying with friends in the meantime. We talked through how they would tell the children and how they'd each arrange to have ample time with the children.

Two weeks later, Jemaine had moved a couple of blocks away. The women reported that the children seemed to be handling things well. They were full of questions, primary among them: "Who will take care of us?" Assured that both moms would continue doing that, the children relaxed a bit and plunged into a process of negotiating who'd go where when. They were establishing a complex rhythm, times when all three were together with each parent, alternating with times when the kids had the option of some separation from each other and chances to be alone with each parent. This latter arrangement turned out to be a real benefit of the split; the twins especially had never been apart, and they began to relish some individual attention.

Over the next months, we negotiated details of money and child custody. What distinguished the work was that each session began with one or another of the partners raising something emotional. Gayle remained unsure about why Jemaine had given up on the relationship. With guidance, she formulated questions that led to clarifying responses from Jemaine, opportunities for her to name, without rancor or judgment, the list of dynamics between them that had worn her out. Jemaine was unwilling to hear very much of Gayle's grief at this stage, and Gayle needed my help guiding the conversation in a way that didn't turn distress into accusation. But together we were able to travel these narrow emotional channels in a way that gave both women enough comfort that they were able to settle their business and move on separately.

Simon and Noreen, on the other hand, landed in my office with a very loud crash. Simon had discovered that Noreen was having an affair, and he was righteously livid. Noreen defended herself by harking back ten years to a similar betrayal by Simon in the first period of their relationship. "I was able to forgive you," she declared. "Why can't you do the same now?"

Simon had moved out on the immediate heels of his discovery. "It's the lying I can't stand," he said, voice shaking. "How can I ever trust you again? At least I confessed to you, but I had to find out by reading your email."

"That's what I can't forgive."

Noreen reported that their two children, teenage girls of thirteen and fifteen, were having very different reactions to their dad's departure. The older girl was furious at him, the younger at her. They were quarreling with each other, each arguing her case against the other parent. The family was in serious disarray.

To make matters worse, Noreen and Simon had declared bankruptcy eighteen months before. With no credit and no savings, they had no idea how to manage a divorce.

It seemed clear to me that an extended divorce mediation was bound for disaster, given the intensity of feeling between them. So we made a short list of the immediate things they'd need to decide in order to stay away from each other for several months, long enough for Simon's rage and Noreen's defensiveness to abate. We came up with a plan for each parent to stay with a friend for a week at a time, rotating out of their current home, arranging dates mid-week with the girls directly (rather than through each other, their more familiar course), and choosing a mutual friend to act as an intermediary should business arise needing immediate attention. We thought through details—birthdays coming up, parties they might both want to attend, the girls' sports events—and divvied them up as equitably as possible.

Finally, we made an appointment four months later to begin working through more permanent arrangements. I suggested they do some reflection in advance, perhaps in conversation with friends or counselors, to recognize feelings that might arise unbidden and derail the mediation. "Write those down," I proposed, "and bring your notes with you. We can deal with the most potentially-explosive things, to get them out of the way of the settlement that you need to negotiate."

Much later, I knew, they might want to do a more thorough-going conversation about their relationship, paving the way to forgiveness and a more peaceable future. But the time for that was not now. More often than not, time helps to heal. Relief from the tensions of a relationship provides a foundation for rebuilding and at some point understanding the reasons why a couple moved apart provides helpful tools.

after the dust settles

Here are eight common post-divorce questions and some ways to approach answers:

- *Is it better for the children to stay in the family home while parents rotate in and out, or for the kids to move back and forth between two households?*

I've seen families handle questions of habitation both ways. In general, my impression is that parents last no longer than a year moving in and out of the house to care for kids, and that year is fraught with strain.

In the first drama of a break-up, parents often think it will be easier on the children to disrupt their lives as little as possible. Depending on the age of the children, the degree of verbal communication customary in the family, the distance between parental households, and a host of other variables, that assessment may or may not be true. Remember the notion of Rescue? It's downfall is its tendency to promote the view that the person being Rescued is a Victim. That is, if parents see the children as delicate and in need of protection at the cost of substantial self-sacrifice, they may communicate to the kids that the situation is scarier than it needs to be in reality.

In short, it's wise to see children as reasonably resilient and yourself as deserving of a little ease as well. If you set things up in a way that heightens your distress, that may be more detrimental to your children's well-being than the disruption of their living arrangements. Seeing you get on your feet, feeling both parents' progress toward increased happiness, more than compensates for the disquiet that comes from moving from household to household.

- *At what intervals should transitions from one parent's care to the other's take place?*

This is a place where it might be possible to consult children's wishes. On the other hand, logistical issues may decide the question. Sid works a super-heavy full-time schedule; Adeline freelances and can choose her own hours. A rigid determination that they split the week down the middle, kids and backpacks on the road every Wednesday and every other Saturday, let's say, makes little sense. Maybe Adeline would prefer to trade free weekends for more weekdays with the kids. Maybe Sid could arrange some flex-time at work, making a late start on Thursdays so he can have a mid-week night with the children.

The rules I proposed in an earlier chapter for negotiation are really important around these sorts of decisions. Everyone needs to start by saying exactly what she or he wants. After the best creative thinking produces ideas that come as close as possible to satisfying those wants, compromises should be crafted with care and flexibility.

One schedule that seems to satisfy many families is a week at each parent's home, with the non-resident parent having at least one date night mid-week. But it you can't stand the thought of going so long without bedtime stories and kisses, the distances between drinks may be too long.

What we know doesn't work is unpredictability. For the sake of everyone's sanity, produce a schedule that can be mapped. Create a calendar, make two copies, and post them on both refrigerator doors. If your children are young (or you yourself have a tilt toward disorganization), color code the thing so it's obvious at a glance who goes where when. Make changes easily evident. Even a very young child should be able to figure out with minimal difficulty where he or she is supposed to be at any given time.

Once you finally have a system that works, expect someone's needs to change. As kids grow older, as parents begin new relationships, as work demands shift, as grandparents become ill, it all needs to be up for renegotiation.

- *What are good ground rules for parental interaction during transfers of kids or at other times in their presence?*

Keep the interaction spare and simple. If you're upset, control yourself until a different time. Handing over tired kids and over-full backpacks at the front door is not a time to air your latest grievance or to open negotiations for a significant change in your agreements.

On the other hand, if something emotionally disruptive is up for you, or if you have a compelling need for renegotiation, you do need to make a time to deal with those problems as soon as humanly possible, lest the energy of upset seep into other, banal transactions. Email is a handy way to notify your ex that you need a conference, but be cautious about dumping emotionally on screen. Email is a flat medium; it conveys emotion with no nuance or human connection, making the receipt of a charged message particularly intense. You might write, "I'd like an hour without kids around to work something through with you," or whatever the agenda is. But don't go into the details, don't write a brief, don't lay out a new program for money and kids that appears, all neatly typed into the computer, to be a *fait accompli.*

It's very helpful to have regularly scheduled times to compare notes about how the kids are doing, how the arrangements are working. You may be too distraught to do that right away, but take your emotional pulse and note the earliest possible time to institute such check-ins. Heading conflict off before it brews into a storm really pays off in the end.

• *What about distinct differences of rules in each parent's household?*

Parent #1 parks kids in front of the TV and does little or no monitoring of what they watch; parent #2 has strict rules about "screen time": how much and what kind. Parent #1 keeps a vegetarian kitchen; parent #2 is a joyous carnivore. Parent #1 is highly organized, insisting that the children stay on top of what clothing they need washed for the next day and establishing a clear and successful routine for ensuring that notes from school and homework assignments come home. Parent #2 has a habit of doing things at the last minute, in a fairly scattered fashion; while s/he sometimes gets annoyed at the kids for following suit, s/he would rather be loose than anxious.

You'd expect kids might get rule-whiplash from all these contradictions. In reality, even very young children generally recognize and accept reasonably quickly that the different households work differently. Some may, of course, use those differences politically: "Dad lets us watch whatever we want. I want to spend more time over there!" Contrasting family cultures give kids more bargaining power. If Dad allows uncensored TV access, Mom may have to make a more persuasive argument about why she does not, and perhaps together she and the child will come up with redeeming features at her house: trips to the library and more allowance for book purchases; more time spent together playing games; more help with homework; a shared project like a kitchen garden.

In this arena like most others, what's necessary is clarity and the avoidance of unending warfare, between the parents and with the kids. Many times, I've seen the adults get locked into a hopeless battle over television. No one ever wins and no one is willing to give up a righteous cause. I would argue that the fight is a greater harm to kids than any particular television program. There is benefit in kids' learning early in life that there are many ways to consider a question, and more than one right answer. It's better to say, "Dad and I do things differently. We don't always agree about things, because we both have strong arguments for how we want things to be. So you get to be two different ways in the two households, and can eventually form your own opinions."

- *How should profound disagreements about key issues—choice of schools, medical care, religious practices, and so on—be handled?*

These are the hard conflicts that probably existed before (and maybe partially led to?) the divorce and are all the more potent now. Hard to resolve because satisfactory compromises are improbable, they involve deep-seated beliefs and values. They hook fear, alienation, and, above all, an angry need for control.

This last sensation is the place to start. When negotiations about religious practices, dietary rules, educational decisions, and other big-ticket items are platforms on which to conduct endless power struggles between divorced parents, no one can win. What can you do to detach your interest in winning from your best effort to act in the interest of your child? Consult trusted others—ideally people who do not themselves tend to fall into the role of allying with you in your war with your ex—and pose the question directly: How do you see me using this conflict as a way to assert my suffering at the hands of my ex? How can I refocus on the question at hand, on the actual child involved and what would be best for her or him?

Exposure to a variety of religious practices can be beneficial for many children, unless each parent asserts her or his own views to be the only right ones. Can you make a distinction between your own dedication to a particular form of spirituality and your recognition that good people may hold other views? Can you trust your child to come to wise beliefs about ethical and theological questions without your having to proselytize or debate? I'm proposing a different sort of act of faith: confidence that you've so empowered your child to embrace positive values that you can lean back rather than forward in directing matters in this arena. Similar principles apply about diet, dress, friends, and a host of other issues.

Medical intervention can induce a more difficult disagreement if life-altering matters should challenge your children. At a moment of dire need, disagreements have a way of surfacing, just when parents are at their most fearful and therefore likely to be in their least negotiable frame of mind. Although no parent wants to forecast bad medical events, it's wise to think through potential scenarios in advance. Think of it as insurance: the more prepared you are, the less likely you'll need it and, if you do, the happier you'll be you've taken care of business. Try to define the range of differences you might encounter: Do you have a philosophical resistance to surgery? How about setting broken bones? Diagnostic X-rays? Antibiotics and long-term medication? Does one of you turn toward western medicine while the other leans east? The more you imagine ways that you can honor both parents' wishes the better. It's an enormous help to have formed positive relationships with health care personnel you trust way in advance of an emergency need for them. Be sure that you both take children to routine appointments so you both get a sense of the trustworthiness of your practitioners. Advice to form good working relationships with health providers runs smack into the dire state of health care in the U.S., of course. If you're not insured (and far too many families are not), you may not have access to consistent care.

Most families are never tested by charged medical situations, but very many do fall out around choices of schools. When Sarah's parents found themselves locked in disagreement about their daughter's high school prospects, they consulted a family counselor for help. Dad, a professor, wanted the best possible academic prospects open to Sarah, a child of keen intelligence. Mom, a therapist and musician, was equally focused on nurturing Sarah's creativity. Their choices were a high-academic private high school, a large proportion of whose graduates gained acceptance at ivy-league universities, or a highly-regarded public school of the arts. Sarah herself was torn: her heart yearned toward the arts school, but she shared her dad's worries that she might later regret some foreclosed academic opportunity.

The counselor referred them to a private educational advisor. A man experienced in helping families facing this quandary, he asked parents and child to grant him the power to arbitrate their decision. Unlike in mediation, where decisions are left to the participants with guidance from the professional, in this case the arbitrator would make the decision. He interviewed each of them in detail. He visited Sarah's current school and talked extensively with teachers and administrators. He visited each of the high school prospects, sat in classes, researched their philosophies and approaches.

In the end, he came to the clear opinion that Sarah would best prosper in the creative school. Within a year, Dad was blessing that choice, for he could see Sarah blossom, full of joy and excitement. To his surprise, she also was coming home with much better grades than she had in her earlier schooling. Always distressed by academic pressure, Sarah was finding ways to learn through the arts, and it exactly suited her. She went on to be accepted at a very prestigious eastern university where she studied theatre. At this writing, she's heading toward a brilliant career on the stage.

- *When and how should children be introduced to a parent's new lover?*

It's wise to wait until you've got a high degree of certainty this new relationship is a keeper. However children handle the introduction of a new adult into their lives, handle it they must. One child may quickly bond, another may stay cool and distant. Both are performing acts of emotional choice that involve some degree of work. If the new person doesn't stick around, the first may be heartbroken, a visible problem. But the second may less obviously be forming a conclusion that adults are not to be trusted and hearts can not be safely opened to new people. For both types of kids, once you do seek to integrate a partner into your family life, you may find yourselves facing a hard task, an arduous process that strains your new relationship.

Given the prevalence of sexual abuse of children, it is doubly wise to be sure you know who a new love really is before exposing your youngsters to potential harm. Do you have a strong sense yet of how your lover wants to relate to children? Does s/he have kids who will also appear as new family? (The next chapter addresses the subject of blended families.) Do you have reasonable agreement about childrearing philosophy? If you adhere to non-violent parenting, you don't want to discover that the partner believes in striking children at a moment of drama. Figure out way in advance how to reconcile significant differences, or, if that's not possible, whose rules prevail. Disagreement and foggy decision-making in an intense moment of conflict with children is likely to be counterproductive to everyone involved.

- *What information should divorced parents tell each other and when?*

My rule of thumb will be familiar to you from earlier chapters: disclose anything relevant; err on the side of more information rather than less.

After the end of a relationship, however, that guideline is a good deal less clear. "Relevant" for the most part should be judged in terms of the children's well-being. Any change that stands to challenge the children's equilibrium is relevant. It's important for other significant adults to know, both so that they can be prepared to help the youngsters deal with the change, but also because these events may well present an emotional challenge for your ex. It's problematic for parent #2 to learn from the child that parent #1 has a new lover. However amicable a split, whoever initiated the break, news like this most often elicits some troubled emotion: sadness, anger, jealousy, relief, whatever it is, best that the child not feel like its cause and not face having to respond to the parent's first flush of feeling.

Other challenging news may involve a new job (will child support and scheduling agreements need to be renegotiated?), a move to another home (how distant? How will visitation and custody be affected?), or a change of roommates (who is this new person? How safe are my kids?).

Over time, life does move on, bringing with it solutions that may have been evasive at an earlier stage, and also bringing new challenges. New partners and the complex dynamics of blended families fit into both categories.

12

recombination:
step-parenting
and blended families

Step-parenting dilemmas are among the most thorny. I've worked with couples spanning the range of possible problems. A few examples:

A has always wanted children but never managed to be in the right relationship at the right time. Now in her mid-forties, she and **B** have fallen in love. **B** has four children and is still in the midst of a sticky divorce from a very angry ex. His kids are divided: two for mom, two for dad. The anti-dad contingent are determined to freeze **A** out, even though the younger of the two secretly likes her. The pro-dad duo consent to play with **A** but turn a deaf ear if she tries anything even vaguely parental.

Their mom is angry and intrusive. She shows up at the front door early on a Sunday morning with a not-very-essential forgotten garment for a child. She calls the children's father at the last moment, knowing he has plans with **A**, claiming an emergency need for help with child transportation. She insists she's going to every soccer game, every school event, every holiday party, and that it's much too soon for her to interact with **A**, who should therefore be kept away.

A and **B** may be in love, but they're having a really hard time making a relationship work.

C and **D** both have kids, and now they've had another one together. Although they've been a blended family for six years, **D**'s teenage daughter refuses to relate to C. Always polite, the girl simply looks away, answering questions monosyllabically and only coming to life in the presence of her sibs and friends. When D complains to her that she's hurting C's feelings, the teenager expresses surprise and claims to be acting totally normally. C continually demands that D do something, but D can't figure out what more to do and secretly thinks C is being unreasonably demanding.

When E and F got together, E's son was just under four. Both easily assumed they would co-parent. But E had been a very part-time parent before the divorce and now was busily engaged in courting the child's favor, applying the age-old principle, "Whatever you want is good by me!"

F loves the youngster but heartily disapproves of such laissez faire parenting. In compensation, F takes on the task of imposing discipline. Whenever a "No" is required, it quickly becomes F's job. E simply looks the other way while F plays the heavy.

Now that the child is an adolescent, F is thoroughly in the doghouse. The teenager screams at F, "I hate you!" and, worse still, "You're not my parent. You can't tell me what to do. I don't have to do what you say!"

Meanwhile, E runs back and forth between the two trying ineffectually to make peace. E and F have long since experienced bed death, and both secretly entertain fantasies of peaceful singleness.

Each of these scenarios involves power dynamics spinning out of control. Agendas and feelings among the adults both fuel and in turn are fueled by dynamics with the children. Step-parenting is proverbially the hardest of relationships to build successfully. For many of the millions who start over again with children in the equation, that folkism proves woefully true.

Of course, there are the counter-stories: G who has no birth children but becomes the closest adult to H's child; I who addresses problems with J's children that have gone unattended for years while I's previous marriage crumbled; **K** who struggled with **L**'s kids for years only to be rewarded with a close and loving connection when the children reached young adulthood.

Generalized advice about these situations is perilous. Familiar though the overall scenario may seem, each situation is actually complex and particular, warranting thorough understanding and strategizing. Ideally, all the involved adults can come to a rapprochement, out of a shared commitment to the well-being of the children. But history may interfere. Among the divorcing couple(s), who left whom and how? If the new liaison predated the break-up, hard feelings may infect relationships for decades to come. Is there an on-going battle over money? Is an ex suffering financial hardship as needed funds flow into a new family? Are grandparents and other kin fuming in the background, unrelenting in their rage at the departed spouse even when the now-divorced partner is struggling to move on from anger?

Similarly, the nuances of cross-generational relationships matter greatly. Every child is different, every parent–child relationship special. So, too, are relationships among siblings, leading sometimes to alliances, other times to contests.

If there are any rules of thumb to consider, try these:

- First, forgive yourself for not knowing how to conduct this welter of confusing, emotion-laden relationships. You're not alone in your quandaries and failures.
- Next, don't hurry things. You and your partner may be experiencing the powerful elixir of new love, choosing each other and jointly deciding to make a new family. But the sense of power accompanying these events for you is probably not shared by the children, and almost certainly not by the divorced spouse(s). Give everyone time to form the relationships that work for them: No pre-cut patterns, no boiler-plates or hide-bound rules.
- Third, do everything you can to de-escalate fights with your now non-resident co-parent. That doesn't mean leaning over backward

to appease her or him; like the Second World War, hostilities are often intensified by undue compromise for the sake of peace. The guidelines for negotiation I've suggested throughout this book are especially important now. Everyone's needs should be articulated, with the understanding that everyone's rights are to be respected. The job of creative resolution may be multiplied by a factor of ten, now, but it still needs to be the goal.

- Consult the children in the new arrangements to the greatest extent possible and appropriate. That is, don't burden children by giving them choices that involve favoring one parent over another, and be scrupulously honest about where your own power of choice is limited. The court may dictate custodial arrangements, and there are likely to be limits to your ability to alter them. Work schedules may be impossible to negotiate among parents; they may now have multiplied several times over (if your new mate has a co-parent, and your ex's new partner has a co-parent, and maybe each of those "co's" is negotiating new romance, the possibilities for scheduling conflicts are manifold!). Nonetheless, the more information is shared and decisions negotiated, the less conflict there will be down the line.

- Don't assume that as a new adult in the family equation you deserve respect and obedience simply by virtual of your position. Assuming a parental role with expectations attached is a perilous proposition. Expect, instead, to build respect slowly over time, by virtue of the wise and wonderful person you are.

Myths and folktales often express a hard nugget of truth; I've often thought the wicked stepmother story a parable of Rescue-Persecution dynamics. Another frame for thinking about the dilemmas confronting a new step-parent is middle management. In discussing parenting teens, I cited research demonstrating that the most stressful position a person can hold is one with lots of responsibility and very little power. That's where many step-parents find themselves. If the biological parent is shying away from confrontation with either the children or the divorced co-parent, the step-parent may be left with a laundry list of hard-to-accomplish tasks: making sure that kids do what they need to do without clear information about what that is; planning ahead for vacations and holidays while cut off from direct communication with an important party to the process; taking on an undue amount of shuttling kids back and forth in order to protect angry divorcees from direct friction with each other. Above all, the step-parent may hold an emotional burden. Often, the divorced partner cannot afford to feel all the anger and sadness potentially there, because to do so would interfere with the necessities of every day diplomacy (or so the person may believe). The other partner may then take on the repressed emotion, hating the ex-spouse, spouting outrage, demanding that the new mate take a hard line and "Stand up for your rights!!"

I see this stance as an emotional Rescue (and a good example of one of those Rescues that springs from powerlessness), and the more it happens, the more the passive parent may lose touch with her or (more commonly) his emotional truth. Now, he or she has to be careful not to exacerbate two angry co-parents' anger. Shuttling back and forth between demanding significant others, s/he finds an authentic emotional voice more and more elusive. The less this parent can speak up independently, the more competitive the two others grow with each other. A sort of phantom war grows steadily more intense: two dynamos warring each other through a mute intermediary, who is increasingly a target for wrath as well.

I've mediated extended families in this state. A first step may be some resolution of history for the divorced couple. But as soon as is advisable, it really helps for the old spouse and the new one to open direct lines of communication. Sometimes, the precipitating event for such peace-making comes from a child. A youngster in distress is taken to a therapist who quickly determines that the child is being torn in many directions by adults in disarray. The child's well-being demands change among the grown-ups, and love for the child may be the only thing powerful enough to induce all the parents to pull together.

Perhaps that's the final guideline I can offer here: if a step parent is having difficulty connecting with a child, look up from that drama to the surrounding adult tensions and start there. Parenting is the hardest work any of us will ever do, given the conditions of scarcity I've named throughout this book. Step-parenting can either relieve those conditions, providing more resources, more adults, and more homes than existed before. But it can also compound the stresses and make the work all the more treacherous. Seek wisdom and help from those who have gone before to find your own particular routes through the thickets.

13

siblings and violence:
fighting and bonding

Is sibling rivalry inevitable? One of the most frequent problems my clients bring to therapy is how to handle all of the squabbling, fighting, teasing, and brutalizing that goes on between siblings. Emotionally, these parents most often appear weary and resigned. With uniformity, most people assume that siblings will fight, that it's an expression of innate aggression. "'Mine!,'" said one mom, "is the first word my kids seem to learn!"

I find it more useful to think of these dynamics in terms of conflict rather than rivalry. "Rivalry" suggests something more endemic, something without solution or end, whereas "conflict" has a cause and, at least sometimes, a resolution. If it's rivalry, then the question is how to tamp it down. The underlying assumption is a need to live with it. Conflict, on the other hand, allows us to ask more productive questions.

What is it that's in conflict? What are children fighting for? Is there some way to get them what they want, rather than socializing them to accept some sort of scarcity that is painful enough to cause them to brutalize each other?

All these questions assume that harming another person is neither natural nor inevitable. In fact, it takes some doing to overcome bonding instincts, I believe, and turn human behavior to destruction. Human potential for kindness is at least as great as for nastiness. Therefore, when children are unkind to each other, we need to figure out why.

Recently, I found myself in a car with my sister and my mother. I asked my sister what she remembered of our sibling relationship growing up. "Miserable!" she said. "I hated you."

I was stung. She's my big sister, barely two years older than me, but throughout my childhood easily the most significant human being in my universe. I was hurt, but quite honestly I was not surprised. "Why?" I asked. "Do you remember?"

Without a moment's thought she said, "You were always there. I could never get rid of you."

We paused for reflection. My sister was driving, our almost-ninety-year-old mother in the passenger's seat beside her. From the back, I went on, "I remember fighting all the time and never knowing why. Maybe now I understand it better."

My mother said, "You girls never fought."

Both my sister and I were stunned. We fought *constantly*. "How can you say that," I exclaimed. "I remember your saying we made the household totally unlivable with our constant fighting."

"Well, you *argued*," said Mom, "but I wouldn't call that *fighting*."

The distinction she made was between sticks and stones on the one hand, and words on the other. It's true we rarely drew blood, but it did become physical (slaps and pinches and scratches), and it was tormenting, both for us and for the adults around us.

My mother's tendency to diminish these dynamics in her recollection is quite common. Fighting among children becomes normalized. My partner, Mariah Breeding, studied sibling violence. The most dramatic dynamic she observed, both in its near-universality and in its impact on the children, was the degree to which adults dismissed the importance of the conflict. "Boys will be boys," daughters were counseled. "What did you do to provoke him?"

There is much about interactions between gender and power ingrained in kids through the process of sibling conflict. Mariah's research showed a complex directionality. It isn't just brothers hurting sisters;

there were many sisters in her study who battered younger siblings, too. But the nature of the interaction was more physical, more severe and more pregnant with messages about male and female access to power when brothers punished sisters. Parents' reactions, or their lack thereof, magnified the effects, and they often blamed the girls, in ways subtle or overt, for the problem.

Not normalizing children's violence toward each other, however, means taking on a Sisyphean task. In the Simmons family (from Chapter Four), when Jimmy and Jenny fought, their mom Julia tried intervention strategies to the point of exhaustion. She would chastise Jimmy, comfort Jenny, tutor Jenny to fight back, try to distract Jimmy. Inadvertently, she suggested to Jimmy he was a "bad boy" (even though she'd do anything to avoid actually saying those words!) and she communicated to Jenny that she was a victim.

Both these notions contained an emotional kernel of truth that made the gender messages all the more persuasive: Julia was angry at Jimmy for his stubborn insistence on "bad" behavior, and many a time she wished Jenny would stop crying and just leave him alone. Nonetheless, she had no intention of characterizing either child; she just didn't know what else to do. Not to intervene might have conveyed the message that Jimmy was entitled to brutalize his sister, and that his sister's mission in life was to manage his feelings. Julia felt between a rock and a hard place. Worse yet, she oscillated between resentment toward the children and self-loathing for her ineffectiveness.

Some reasons for children to fight seem fairly clear. While grown ups tend to define these conflicts in terms of competition for parents' attention, my experience of it is much more in line with my sister's comment: younger kids want to have everything to do with older ones; older ones simply want freedom from interference, at least some of the time. Siblings both are and are not peers. They are, of course, closer in age and circumstance to each other than to their parents. But they are also unequal in lots and lots of ways. A two-year difference in age makes a huge difference in development, especially early in life. A two-and-a-half year old is walking, talking, building, drawing, play acting, and more. An eight-month old is crawling and grabbing for the older child's carefully placed toys—and maybe teething and cranky: in short, being a pest.

At the same time, children are social creatures. They want playmates. Grown ups are a poor substitute for other children. No wonder Jenny keeps going back to Jimmy, and no wonder Jimmy keeps rebuffing her.

In an ideal world, there would be lots of peers for both children. My Indian village model is helpful, where packs of kids of all ages play together constantly. There is very little conflict among the children, for there's always someone for each one to engage.

So what do you do within the four walls of your isolated home? (All right, I won't repeat my repeated advice, which is to find a more peopled way to live!) To the extent you can, distract the younger child with other sources of entertainment. Reason with the older child, suggesting, perhaps, that Jimmy play with Jenny for awhile during which time he teaches her something new (thereby acknowledging Jimmy's greater skill and knowledge), and that you'll then take Jenny away so Jimmy can play peacefully with his own toys for awhile.

It's also helpful to speak the truth: "Sorry, Jimmy. I know she's pestering you. How about if I hang out with you for a bit, and we try to invent a new game that's fun for both of you?"

The companion statement is, "I know you want to play with Jimmy, Jenny. He's really neat, isn't he? But sometimes he wants to play alone (or with the kids next door). So here's something you can do in the meantime, until he's ready to play with you."

The most damaging thing you can do is ignore the problem. The least effective thing you can do is scold either or both of the children. The greatest power you have is to adopt a positive view of the children's behavior, dignifying their reactions and desires, and framing what's going on in those terms to them as well as to yourself.

beyond annoyance

Sometimes, however, fighting between siblings goes beyond the level of Jenny and Jimmy, or of my sister and me. Sometimes serious damage happens.

While I'm advocating taking all conflict among kids seriously, I think it's also important to name the difference between degrees of violence and other forms of abuse. Without any physical act, a child can humiliate and torment a sibling psychologically. Sexual predation happens among children, and sometimes the line between this form of abuse and positive childhood sexual exploration confuses adults. Indeed, tormenting a sister or brother can take as many inventive forms as human creativity permits.

There are times, in other words, when it's necessary simply to put a stop to harmful behaviors. "No, Jimmy, you may not choke your sister!" Physical intervention may be necessary if a child is being hurt. I've known parents to be forced to send a son to live with relatives rather than to allow the possibility of continuing sexual abuse of a younger child.

One of the most moving stories I've heard adults tell about their experiences along these lines is about the intervention of an adult outside the family. If parents cannot or will not do what's needed, an aunt or uncle, a neighbor or teacher may have to blow the whistle.

For some families, violence is a fact of life between the adults as well as the children. A parent who is being physically assaulted by another adult is likely to be less able to intervene between warring children. Witnessing adult-on-adult violence may incline children in one of two directions: to make stronger alliances with each other, or to manifest the pain and stresses of a violent household in cruel behavior toward each other. Sometimes, of course, both patterns weave in and out of each other.

Adult-on-child violence may also lie behind serious sibling assault. To pass the humiliation and powerlessness experienced as the victim of physical punishment down the line is a major way in which hierarchies get established and perpetuated.

Needless to say, everything I've written in this book is gainsaid by any form of violence within the family. Fear of physical damage makes impossible the kinds of cooperative power sharing that I'm advocating. The first step toward any positive change is for the violence to stop— reliably and totally. That usually means the perpetrator of violence needs to accept responsibility, to make a clear decision to foreswear any form of violence ever again, and to have a practical and effective plan for what to do when any temptation to be violent reoccurs. A plan may involve enrolling in some anti-violence program. It certainly requires a commitment to call for help when in jeopardy. Although violence is often experienced as a split-second occurrence, it is not. People typically say, "I saw red, and it was out of my control." But from working with people learning to manage violent behavior, we know with a good deal of certainty that there is a moment when one makes a decision to let fly. Often that decision is bolstered by a justification: "She provoked me; I'm so stressed and exhausted I'm entitled to lash out." Thoughts like these need to be reconstructed and reconsidered as part of the work of embracing non-violence. Family violence prevention programs have had a lot of success working with men who batter partners. So we know that violence can be stopped.

I believe there is a web of connections from home to the world. How we are as members of society shapes how we are with loved ones, and vice versa. One of the more destructive ideas I hear from people is that home is the place we get to let it all hang out, that it's somehow all right to trash family members after restraining anger out in the world all day long. I believe exactly the opposite – not that we should go around trashing others outside the home, but that we need to be our most lovingly disciplined precisely with those we love the most. Otherwise, the strong bonds of intimacy get torn apart, and what should be the most empowering and healing of relationships become the most insidiously destructive.

I'm not suggesting that peace at home translates in a simple way into peace in the Middle East. But I do strongly believe that violence at home seriously undermines any possibility of bringing about peace in the world. Paradoxically, so much domestic violence flows from oppression experienced in other parts of our lives. People who are treated badly at work, who do meaningless jobs, who are exposed daily to discrimination, or who live daily on the edge of economic insecurity and self-doubt are hardly in the best shape to be generous and disciplined at home.

14

death in the family:
growing through
the states of life

With any kind of luck, the first death your children confront will be a pet. I don't mean to be heartless, nor "humanist." The loss of an animal is enormously sad and grieving can be as deep and pervasive as for a person.

But in many families the death of a pet is less mystified to kids than the death of a family member or friend. Children are more likely to witness an elderly animal's decline into illness. You may feel less need to protect youngsters from your conversation about what's going on, as well as about end-of-life decisions you must make. In modern industrialized society, animals die at home more often than humans do. Children can be present, petting the dog or cat, waiting and watching as it (hopefully) gently breathes its last. The family may gather in the backyard to dig a grave, invent a ritual, and lay the pet to rest. All of those experiences are very material, involving children in tactile acts and shared emotions.

Human deaths, however, are for most children exceedingly abstract. I know, that's a weird thing to say about something as concrete, as definitive as death. But young kids have great trouble grasping the concept of finality. Most things in their experience are, in fact, cyclical. Grandma comes to visit, goes away, and then comes back again. Uncle so-and-so

lives in another city; he only appears at Thanksgiving dinner and occasional, unexpected other times.

Told that her grandfather had died, Jenny, three years old at the
time, put on a sad face for she could see that her mother, Julia, was
grieving. A tear rolled down the child's cheek. "Where is he now?" she
asked somberly, channeling her mother's sadness.

"He's gone to heaven," Julia replied.

"Will he be back in time for Christmas?" asked Jenny.

That "gone" means "not here right now but coming back soon" to
a three-year-old is fully consistent with a child's experience of life. So
how do you then make sense for her of *your* grief, a sadness far more
intense than can be explained by the child's concept of "gone"? For a
very small child, "Mommy's sad because she misses Grandma" may be
sufficiently explanatory. But if mommy is still sad six months later, the
child may wonder why since grandma may not have appeared in her
life more frequently than that anyway.

The more said about the emotions surrounding the death of a loved
one, the better. Once again, discretion is required. Letting children know
you are sad is different from loud wailing in the child's presence. There
is a balance needed between feeling and language, so that the youngster
is informed but not burdened. Another place for balance is in telling a
child how s/he can help, while at the same time being careful not to
impose a worrying need for a little one's support: "Come give Mommy
a hug. There, now I feel much better." Mourning is an opportunity to
teach something about both the journey that is emotion and the power
of a child to participate. We are capable of feeling deeply, and through
the very experience of that feeling we change and move on.

Often, the loss of a grandparent is a child's first exposure not only to
a significant death, but also to a parent's profound emotion. I remember,
at the age of twelve, carefully watching my father to assess his reactions
to his father's loss. It was a wonderment to me that this big, powerful
man was shaken. But I remember also feeling critical that he was nei-

ther sobbing nor rending his clothing. He was curiously matter of fact as he went about funeral arrangements and the other business of death. I realized that my father was, first, more vulnerable than I had known him to be, and, second, less capable of a sort of emotional expression that was, for me, represented by exaggerated dramatizations. Lacking a lot of open language for feeling in my home, I had formed my ideas about mourning in the movie theatre. But real life was certainly not following art at that moment.

expectation is a two-way street

The other side of my skewed expectation about how my father's grief should manifest, is the worried anticipation adults often have about what their children feel. Daniel's cousin lived across the continent, in a small suburban community very different culturally from the urban environment in which Daniel had grown up. The two boys were close in age, but they saw each other at best once a year and they'd never gotten along very well.

When the cousin was fifteen, he committed suicide. Daniel's parents were devastated, especially his father whose sister was the mother of the deceased boy. While consoling the mother and working through his own deep sense of shock, guilt ("Why hadn't I noticed something was wrong last summer when we visited?!"), and grief, Daniel's father was also dealing with terror. He scrutinized Daniel closely for signs of depression. He read every Web article he could find about suicide contagion among teenagers. He consulted counselors about how to help his son grieve, lest his feelings turn inward and induce suicidality.

And indeed, Daniel seemed distant and unfeeling, appearances that the Web writings suggested were symptomatic. At length, his parents brought him to me to see what repressed reactions I might shake loose.

"Honestly," Daniel said shyly, "I didn't like my cousin very much. He was way more macho than I am, and he teased me endlessly for wanting to read a book.

"I know it's very sad, and I can see my dad is freaked out. But what's really got *me* down is that I'm getting a bad grade in math this marking period—I haven't wanted to tell my parents about it because I know they'll be upset, and they're already upset enough. But I'm really miffed and also worried about how to bring the grade up."

Suicide is an enduring tragedy when anyone does it, but all the more so when a teenager kills himself. Of all possible deaths, it may be the hardest for survivors to handle, because it always involves some degree of discordance in a relationship. Either people didn't know, or they did and were helpless to stop it. In either case, guilt and a searing sense of powerlessness intensify sadness and loss. Anger, too, can follow a suicide—"Why didn't the little so-and-so ask for help!?"—a feeling quickly chased by new waves of guilt.

But children may be experiencing the death very differently, as Daniel indicated. Not at all suicidal himself, he was more irritated with his parents' over-the-top concern about him than mourning the cousin's loss. Submerged in that dynamic with his parents was his genuine wish to be helpful to them. "I know my dad's really upset, and I'd like to be a comfort to him. But the minute I get anywhere close, he becomes too sad for me to handle and too worried about me. I just have to get away."

death of a parent

The one loss that is not at all abstract to children is the death of a parent or a sibling. The process of death is apt to be much more apparent when it occurs in the household. Although the moment of death may still happen in a hospital, and while children may still be barred from scenes thought to be too distressing for them to handle, it is still much harder to obscure the reality of what's happening when it so changes the reality of day-to-day life.

Again and again throughout this book, I've advocated relationships with children that are both honest and simultaneously cognizant of the power differential between adults and youngsters. In the presence of death, the same thing is true. Children (like adults) have a much better chance of handling hard-to-handle experiences if they can name then, understand them, and share them with other people. The temptation to hide terminal illness from children is understandable, but it backfires. Again and again, I've listened to the pained stories of adults who were never told that a death was impending, who never understood what happened nor had a chance to say good-bye.

I believe it is better to be open about what is happening, and to create an atmosphere in which youngsters can express what they feel to people who are present to comfort and support them. What does ultimately give protection to children is the lived experience of the love and care of other people, both through the process of a parent's dying and afterward. The surviving parent needs the help of as many other caring adults as possible, lest the necessity of meeting a child's needs while dealing with ones own become overwhelming.

The death of a parent shatters a child's confidence in the natural order of the world. Mother and father are supposed to be there to care for their offspring. That is an expectation shared across generations. When death interferes, beyond the immediacy of the child's loss there lies another loss: of a sense that there is order and predictability in the universe. If this bad thing can happen, what other bad things might happen? If the child has no power to intervene now—despite desperate wishes, despite ardent prayers—then what becomes of the child's belief in a benevolent spirit guiding life?

In a *New York Times* story, a young man whose father died when he was ten and his mother nine years later was quoted as saying, "I was very angry with God. He came in and took my father and then he took the other person I loved most in the world."

If this rearrangement of a child's conception of the physical and spiritual universe is profound when a parent dies, it may be even more distressing after the death of a sibling or close friend. Parents are, after all, old from a child's perspective. There is a gulf of generation between the mortality of an adult and a child. That separation vanishes, however, when a child dies. If that can happen to her, then it could happen to me! The fear may become a lot more personal: rather than "Who will take care of me?" it may be "Will I die, too?"

Adults' tendency in such painful circumstances is to be reassuring. "No, you're not sick. You won't die." But children, with their enormous sense of the real, don't buy it. Surely some grown up said the same thing to the child who now lies in the coffin. Fear is better assuaged when it is validated: "You could die. That's true for every person and creature that lives. But most children don't, not until they're very, very old. You are healthy, whereas Johnny had a heart problem from the time he was born. We know your heart is strong; put your hand on it and feel how powerfully it beats. I expect you'll live a long, long time."

a fit conclusion

Maintaining a balance between adult nurturing and honest communication in the face of a death, at a time when we grownups ourselves are at out most distressed, is a significant test of parental development. The ability to communicate, to stay open and clear in the presence of strong emotion, to negotiate needs with both children and co-parents, to handle one's own anxieties without burdening children, to understand and respect the strengths and capabilities of the young, and to stand by them as they embark on their own separate journeys: all these developmental tasks once accomplished come together in the ability to support a child confronting the death of a loved one.

I hope that you need never pass that test, at least, not while your children are small and not until you've all had time to grow and learn the necessary lessons.

15

ending thoughts

I leave you with one last piece of advice: Take this book, and all other advice, and make it your own. Some of what I've written here will apply and be useful, some may spur creative ideas in you – things I've never thought of, ways to be that are wholly right for you and not for another parent. In a sense I'm offering to you the advice I've given you about your kids – to recognize and respect the ways they are their own people, each one unique, each one confronting aspects of life common to all. Be kind and forgiving to yourself. It is a truism that every parent makes some mistakes; I put that statement in the context of the external world we all inhabit. It is a society thick with contradictions. We do the work of parenting with gales of hardship in our faces, as well as kindly winds of support at our backs. There can be no individual perfection in a universe of imperfect sustenance.

As I've prepared this manuscript for publication, I've talked with Josh and Tuhin about how their experience of growing up accords with my reflections here. Tuhin has his own complex memories of collective living. He speaks of his "other parents" with love and respect, and at the same time he has some memories that are painful. We certainly played out our own version of Rescue, Victim, Persecution, different from the ones I've described in this book primarily in the complexity added by the involvement of more people.

Josh's critique is a wise reflection on some of those dynamics. He wishes we had been more clear about the consequences of some of his actions when he was very young. He feels he had less of an inner guide when he hit adolescence, because he didn't really believe there were any consequences that were serious. Partly, that reality might have been the result of ways we Rescued him to compensate for his relative invisibility at school. Partly, it might have been a paradoxical consequence of there being fewer consequences because we lived so much in community and the real consequences of his not doing his chores were spread over many adults. In my sixties, I'm still learning about parenting from my kids.

And some of that learning is about being parent to adult children. Power has shifted, wonderfully. The boys are prospering, finding love and learning and meaning in large portions. I couldn't be prouder of them both. But sometimes I'm confused about my role with them. Should I be insisting on family dinners when they don't fit into their busy schedules (or mine, for that matter)? Where's the line between maintaining family and, simply, my pleasure in their company?

Family dinners go by the by. Quality connection does not. When they are too absorbed in their own lives to make time together, I do a disproportionate share of the calling and inviting. That's a way I'm still Mama, still a reflection of different stages of life and our different roles. I notice, though, that I also call my own mother more than she calls me; that's a change, and I expect to see it following down the generations over time.

I'd like to think I was the perfect parent; wouldn't you? I wasn't, and you won't be. So give yourself a break… and keep growing and learning and trying and changing and loving.

index